Visual Outline Charts of the New Testament

M. Scott Bashoor

Foreword by H. Wayne House

Revised and Expanded

Southern California Seminary Press
El Cajon, California

Visual Outline Charts of the New Testament
Revised and expanded edition

Published by Southern California Seminary Press
El Cajon, CA

ISBN-13: 978-0986444258

Previously published digital version: *Visual Outline Charts of the New Testament* by B&H Academic Digital, Nashville, TN ©2016 from https://wordsearchbible.lifeway.com/.

ENDORSEMENTS

"It is my conviction that the Bible is not difficult for the believing heart to understand. And the more we understand, the more unshakable our conviction that the Bible is the living, authoritative, inerrant Word of God. The more I study it, the more I hunger to know. That is why I am grateful for the efforts of Scott Bashoor and the fine work he has done in producing these outline charts. Their unique style and detailed content provide an excellent study tool for pastors and lay people alike. They are an important resource, and it is my prayer that they will be used by the Lord to bless many."

—John MacArthur, D.D., Chancellor Emeritus, The Master's University & The Master's Seminary

"A visual presentation of the layout and contents of a New Testament book can be so helpful in seeking to keep the "big picture" of the book in mind as one interprets the individual components. M. Scott Bashoor's *Visual Outline Charts of the New Testament* is a trustworthy guidebook for that enterprise, giving just the right amount of detail in the accurate and aesthetically pleasing charts provided for each New Testament book. I am glad to know of this new resource and happy to commend it to others."

—Robert L. Plummer, Ph.D., Collin and Eveyln Aikman Professor of Biblical Studies, The Southern Baptist Theological Seminary; Host, *The Daily Dose of Greek* screencast

"Gaining an accurate overview of a biblical book is an important step in personal Bible study and preparation for preaching and teaching. Scott has performed a great service for busy pastors and serious students of the Bible by providing an attractive visual outline of each book of the New Testament in chart form. This book of charts deserves wide and thoughtful use."

—John D. Grassmick, Th.D., Emeritus Professor of New Testament Studies, Dallas Theological Seminary

"I discovered many years ago that I get more out of a book if someone gives me an overview first. Biblical books are no different. Bashoor has offered the church quite literal "overviews" of New Testament books—visually organized outlines that are simple, clear, and concise. *Visual Outline Charts of the New Testament* will help anyone needing introductions to these precious, divinely inspired writings."

—Mark Ward, Ph.D., Lexham Press

"Although we live at a time when there are an abundance of Bibles, Christians seem to know less of the content of their Bibles than ever before. It is also a time when many believers think of their Bibles more as a collection of disconnected Bible verses than as narratives and letters. Scott Bashoor's volume not only invites readers to get more deeply into their Bibles, but to understand the flow of thought and inner coherence of each New Testament book. The graphical representation of this thought development will greatly assist the learning process."

—Clinton E. Arnold, Ph.D., Dean and Professor of New Testament, Talbot School of Theology, Biola University

"When it comes to jigsaw puzzles, I like to keep the box cover nearby. The box cover provides me the big picture as I work with each individual puzzle piece, it helps me see each piece in connection with the whole. Scott Bashoor's very helpful outline charts work in a similar manner. As you and I grapple with the biblical text they help us keep the big picture, and a clear focus on the author's larger intent. These visuals help us study the New Testament holistically which in turn provides us with a more comprehensive understanding of God's love for us in Christ as revealed in Scripture. I intend to keep this book near my open Bible, and I encourage you to do the same."

—Philip De Courcy, M.Div., Pastor of Kindred Community Church in Anaheim Hills, California; Teacher on the daily radio program *Know the Truth.*

DEDICATION

To Heidi,
whose supportive love and patient perseverance in the Lord's service and life together inspire and encourage my service to Christ each day.

TABLE OF CONTENTS

FOREWORD

When asked to write this foreword for M. Scott Bashoor's *Visual Outline Charts of the New Testament*, I was especially pleased. I love charts, having produced ten charts books over the years. In fact, a charts book on the New Testament was my first book, so it was interesting for me to see an approach that focused on the content of the New Testament different from mine. The allure of charts is that they bring together into a short, organized form a look at more complicated or exhaustive materials so that the user has an introduction to a subject before working through it.

Professor Bashoor has certainly accomplished his task in a masterful way with *Visual Outline Charts of the New Testament*. Each of the books of the New Testament have a brief introductory page in which questions of authorship, purpose, audience, etc., are given. In regard to the actual content of the New Testament books, each of the portions of the New Testament is laid out in an organized format, largely in color, so that the reader receives an overview of each portion of the New Testament that the author presents before delving into each of these books. As one follows Bashoor's guidance from the overview to the detail of the text, the reader is able to grasp the subject matter, structure, emphasis, and argument of each of the Gospel narratives, and apostolic letters. This assists the reader to comprehend the thesis of each book as developed by the biblical author and more easily remember the basic content of each of the books.

I am, therefore, very happy to recommend *Visual Outline Charts of the New Testament*. This work will differ from so many books on the biblical text in which authors write about what a given scholar thinks about each book, or discussion of external information relating to the books. Professor Bashoor's work allows the actual content of the New Testament to be understood by the reader.

—H. Wayne House, M.A., J.D., Th.D., Distinguished Research Professor of Theology, Law, and Culture,
Faith International University and Faith Seminary

PREFACE

The production of *Visual Outline Charts of the New Testament* (VOCNT) has been an unexpected harvest while laboring in the Lord's vineyard. These charts had their beginning in my pastoral ministry in 2014 when I made simpler versions of them as Bible class handouts. Over the years I expanded and modified the charts significantly for classes I taught at The Master's Seminary and later The Master's University.

Admittedly, the greater focus of my academic work relates to the Old Testament. I have taught Semitic languages for over 15 years, and I am pursuing a Ph.D. in OT. That said, it has also been my privilege to teach English Bible courses on New Testament survey, Paul's writings, Revelation, and hermeneutics. Furthermore, my commitment to expository preaching has enabled me to teach through significant portions of the NT verse by verse.

It was a great joy to see a version of these charts first published in 2016 by B&H Academic Digital, and I am grateful that the digital version remains available through Logos Bible Software. Response to the work was heartening, including many who desired to see a paperback version. In December 2017, I released a "Special Print Edition," through an independent platform. While that edition scratched a proverbial itch, self-publication has its limits. For that reason and others, I am thrilled that the print rights have been acquired by SCS Press.

This SCS Press edition contains numerous improvements. Format and color schemes have been enhanced, and the appealing cover invites readers to explore the book. I am especially happy about new introductory text for the NT books. I briefly discuss the major purpose and context of each book and why I prefer the outlining schemes utilized. Some of the new material appeared earlier in articles for *Voice: An Independent Church Journal*, but it has all been adapted for this new edition of VOCNT.

I am deeply indebted to one of my mentors at TMS, Dr. Keith Essex, who has taught English Bible courses for several decades. Some structural and interpretive decisions in VOCNT reflect his studied influence. In the end, however, the work is my own and should be judged as such.

Of course, I am also beholden to so many who have published their labors in NT studies. VOCNT's bibliography is suggestive rather than extensive since my own study for preaching through the years has been informed by many more sources than those listed. Since the nature of this work is one of summary and distillation, the charts themselves are not annotated. I have not intended to be creative in my analysis of texts, only in the presentation of material in visual form.

A few key people have been very helpful in editing. Dwayne Ewers, Dr. Dennis Swanson, and Cynthia Esmond proved invaluable in their editorial suggestions. And most recently, Cory Marsh at SCS Press has been an encouraging editor and promoter.

I am thankful for the faithful people at Community Bible Church for their patience and support through the years and their manifest love of the Word. They are a joy to shepherd.

Finally, I am thankful for my supportive wife, Heidi. What has been a sacrifice of time for me has equally been so for her. Long before a book was ever envisioned, she patiently allowed me to "over study" as I prepared adult Bible classes, sermons, and lectures. We wondered back then whether God would be pleased to use those efforts for something more. We are thankful to see the Lord at work in ways beyond what we have asked or thought.

La Mirada, California

INTRODUCTION

Visual Outline Charts of the New Testament (*VOCNT*) presents single page displays of the structure and content of each book of the New Testament. These charts are intended for pastors, Bible teachers, college and seminary students, and studious Christian readers. Each chart uses shades of color and font changes to guide the eye through the major sections and sub-sections of NT Scripture. While these charts are no replacement for commentaries or other study tools, I hope that they will prove useful for anyone wishing to enhance their understanding of the NT. Below I will explain how to utilize these charts for personal and group use, and point out limitations to this charting system.

How to Read These Charts

Traditional outlines utilize lists of summary statements, often with Roman numerals and indented sub-points. The vast majority of resources I have consulted have included such displays. A visual outline is free to arrange material in a fashion more appealing to the eye. Visual outlines are not just for the visual learner but can help any viewer see the whole scope of material more easily. Of course, there is no single kind of visual outline. There are tables, flowcharts, relationship trees, Venn diagrams, mind maps, and other formats. *VOCNT* utilizes a table format.

Each chart is designed to guide the eye across the page from one major heading to the next, and down into lower rows and columns for further details. Each NT book has one primary chart. Larger books have follow-up, focus charts which drill down into sections with greater detail. The screenshots below illustrate the different parts of the charts.

The top row of the primary charts includes three elements: the book's title (a), a purpose statement (b), and a box with vital background information such as date, authorship, recipients, and other related circumstances (c). The second and third rows reveal the main sections of the book (d). Lighter shaded rows below provide sub-section summaries for each column (e).

Focus charts for larger books follow up on particular parts of the book not detailed in full on the primary chart (a). Various levels of subordination are indicated as follows: level one uses bold, level two uses regular font, level three (when needed) uses italics, and level four (when needed) uses a smaller font. Those major sections that have already been detailed or are yet to be detailed are

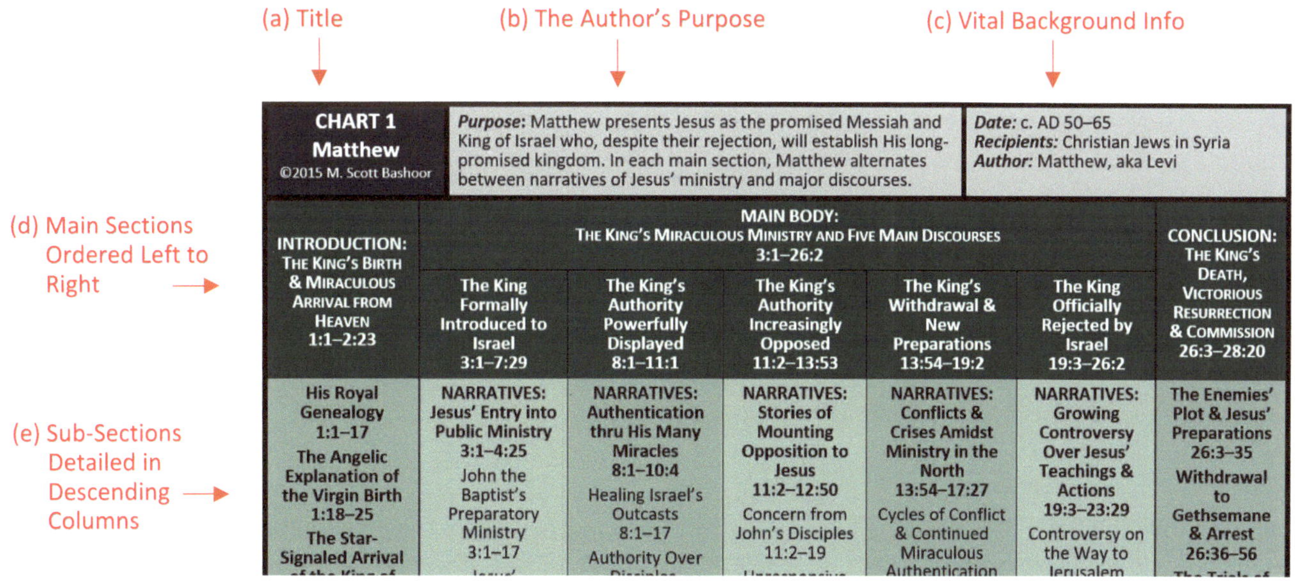

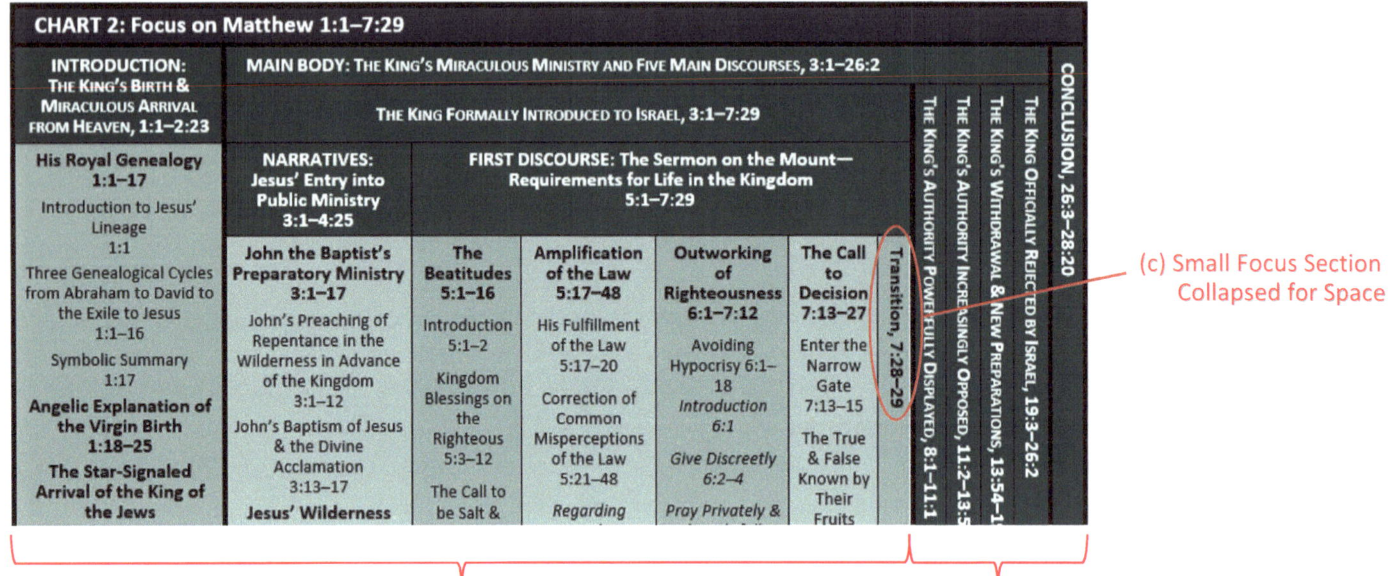

(a) Portion Detailed in Matthew's Chart 2: 1:1–7:29 (b) Collapsed Portions to be Detailed in Subsequent Charts 1:1–7:29

collapsed into vertical columns. This enables the reader to see how the present text fits into the larger flow of the book (b). On occasion, there are small sections in the focus material that have been collapsed for the sake of space (c).

Since the copies of the Greek New Testament contain variant readings including the addition and omission of verses, the reader will occasionally find verse numbers in brackets. I have only incorporated this when disputed verses appear on the edges of sections. In the example to the right from Matthew 18:7–10 [11], verse 11 is bracketed because it is not found in key NT manuscripts and hence is not in most modern translations. Most often these instances involve single verses. On rare occasions there are larger disputed sections such as the long ending of Mark (16:9–20) and the Pericope Adulterae (John 7:53–8:11). These portions have been retained in the outline charts, but they are entirely in brackets.

> The Removal of Stumbling Blocks of Sin 18:7–10 [11]
>
> *Stumbling Blocks in One's Own Life 18:7–9*
>
> *Stumbling Blocks for Others 18:10 [–11]*
>
> The Missing Sheep & God's Pursuit of His Little Ones 18:12–14

The charts are based on my readings of the NT in English. I have worked primarily with the *New American Standard Bible*, though I have kept an eye on the Greek text and other translations. On occasion my differences with the NASB's renderings are evidenced in the ways I have summarized small sub-sections, particularly in the epistles. I encourage readers of these charts to make use of multiple translations, particularly when summary statements seem to be at odds with whatever translation they might be using.

The Appendix provides a few additional charts covering matters such as the now-traditional order of the books in our Bibles, the order of composition of NT books, a chronology of the life of Paul in relation to the books he composed, and an outline of Isaiah 53, the extended OT passage most often quoted or alluded to by NT writers.

How to Use These Charts

The charts are each designed to stand alone. One does not need to look at all the charts to benefit from one chart or one set of charts. Of course, the NT itself is richly interconnected, but these charts are designed as independent reference tools. For instance, one does not need to look at the Matthew charts in order to use the charts for Mark. The following are suggested ways to use *VOCNT* based upon my own experience and the comments of others who have found the charts helpful.

The Pastor's Study

VOCNT can be very helpful to the pastor and Bible teacher as he prepares sermons and Bible studies. If one is preaching an expository series through a book, *VOCNT* can help with planning out the course and pace of preaching.

If preaching topically, *VOCNT* can provide a helpful sense of context to the key passages selected. Topical preaching is sometimes vilified by expositors because of its easy misuse. But it can be a valuable means of teaching biblical truth, and it enriches the listeners most when the selected verses are understood in their contexts.

VOCNT can also help the pastor or Bible class teacher present survey level material in classes and Bible studies. The charts themselves look at texts with a bird's eye view at various levels of altitude.

Curriculum and Classroom Use

VOCNT is a useful resource to include in required reading lists for Bible courses in colleges, seminaries, and Bible institutes. Many survey courses require students to read through the entirety of the NT and submit papers on the content and themes of its books. *VOCNT* can help students follow the authors' flow of thought and better understand the whole of what they are reading. Over the years, I have received substantial feedback from students appreciating the intended purpose, main themes, and key movements outlined in each chart—essential elements to NT study that may have previously been overlooked. *VOCNT* continues to help professors surveying the overall picture of the NT.

The Believer's Personal Study

VOCNT is a potentially enriching tool for the serious student of God's Word working through the text on his or her own. *VOCNT* will be most useful to the student who has read through the biblical material beforehand. Reading through the material again with *VOCNT* open can help explain the flow and structure of the material. The warm color design of each chart conveniently groups three large blocks of NT material to help direct the eyes for an easy-to-follow study outline. Consequently, each chart's accessibility makes a handy aid for personal or group Bible study, and sermon preparation. By way of my own pastoral ministries, *VOCNT* has been tested, refined, and used repeatedly in various church settings, all the while with the reader in mind.

Discipleship Tool

Learning to read and understand the Bible is a key part of discipleship. Many new Christians (and older ones as well) do not understand that all individual passages are part of a larger flow of thought and argument. *VOCNT* can be used in one-on-one or small-group discipleship settings to teach the structures and contents of God's life-transforming Word. The primary charts (book level) might prove especially helpful in this regard.

Limitations of the Charts

VOCNT is an entry-level commentary of sorts, but it is no substitute for other valuable research and study tools. There are many, many things that these charts do not cover, and even the coverage that it provides has its limitations.

Limited Perspective

It goes almost without saying that chapter breaks and verse breaks—those useful tags inserted into our Bibles in the last millennium—are too often misplaced. Commentators have long lamented the sometimes inexplicable, medieval divisions made to the text. *VOCNT* presents my own understandings of the structure. I have not ventured to present understandings unique to myself, but the decisions I have made are all represented by those in the field of NT studies. However, looking at my charts alone does not reveal the existence of other approaches. For instance, the charts on Hebrews conceal the reality that there have been multiple outline approaches that do not concord entirely with my scheme.

There are a number of NT books over which scholars have had long-standing debates about structure. Perspectives often congeal around a few dominant approaches, as with the study of Matthew. In other cases, there is virtually no consensus, as with the study of James. While outlines of numerous books are debated in small ways, I found the debates to be especially involved in the books of Matthew, Luke, Acts, Romans, Hebrews, James, 1 John, and Revelation.

There are many differences of opinion on sub-level divisions as well. While the seams of small passages are usually obvious, sometimes there are transitional verses where it is not clear whether to fit them with the sections before or after. A case in point is Philippians 3:1. Does the "Finally, brethren" indicate the conclusion of the previous section or the beginning of another? My outline follows one line of analysis in this regard, but other interpreters are compelled otherwise.

Another area of dispute involves the purpose statements for each book. For instance, my understanding of Romans is that Paul wrote the epistle to give gospel-based instruction and counsel to Jewish and Gentile Christians who were struggling to relate to one another properly. Others believe that Paul's primary purpose in writing the book is to make a strategic deposit of gospel truth in the heart of the empire. Still others see Paul's primary purpose as theologically preparing the church at Rome to support him in a major mission he envisioned for the western side of the empire. These purposes are not necessarily exclusive to one another, but my chart has selected one theme as dominant.

Even some of the vital background information material in the primary charts is disputed by conservative scholarship. For instance, I have followed the traditional dating for the Gospel of Mark, placing it around AD 64–68. This would make Mark the third gospel produced. Contemporary scholarship generally favors Mark as the first gospel written, but these charts do not contain space to debate such issues.

Since I am committed to the Reformation principles of *Sola Scriptura* (Scripture alone) and *Semper Reformanda* (always reforming), I expect that my own understanding of NT texts will evolve—hopefully for the better—as I progress in the faith and the Lord's service.

Limited Space

Not only is there not enough space in the charts to alert the reader to alternative approaches, sometimes space is lacking to analyze portions as thoroughly as I might have liked. The reader will find some unevenness in the level of detail when comparing charts of some books with others. Form has limited function, but I trust not in intolerable ways.

VOCNT limits every chart to a single page, a formatting commitment that sometimes requires great brevity. Commentaries often provide lengthy sentences to summarize major sections, but the summaries in *VOCNT* range between one to twelve or so words. I have tried to break down all passages (eventually) into units no larger than a dozen or so verses. Many passages are broken down much further, sometimes even into single verse divisions.

There are places in the NT where authors have utilized chiasmus, but I am not yet convinced of their presence on macro-syntactical levels. Were I to be persuaded of such, I would create supplemental charts to provide a visual display. Many micro-level chiasms are generally at a level too small to be represented in these charts.

Adherents to various forms of rhetorical analysis will no doubt be disappointed by the lack of much reference to rhetorical elements in these charts. There are some instances where I have cued into oratorical features, as in Hebrews, but the charts do not have much room to develop these concepts where they may be present.

Conclusion

With the above suggestions and limitations in mind, readers can gain or refresh their understandings of the flow and content of NT books as they read through *VOCNT* with an open Bible. May the Lord be pleased to use this book to aid those exploring the still uncharted depths of the love of the Savior who has inspired the New Testament by his Spirit.

THE NEW TESTAMENT WRITINGS

The New Testament is the collection of Spirit-inspired writings from the first century AD which complete the Bible. These documents are centered around the person, work, and legacy of the Lord Jesus Christ covering both His earthly sojourn and His heavenly ministry. This library of writings fulfills the aims of the Old Testament compiled centuries before. Unlike the Old Testament which was written over a 1000-year period (c. 1400 BC–400 BC), the New Testament was written over a 50-year period (c. AD 40–AD 95). This era saw an explosion of spiritual activity surrounding the first coming of Jesus, the promised Messiah. The New Testament presents Jesus Christ as the fullest and final revelation of God, fulfiller and mediator of ancient promises to Israel, and the bearer of light and salvation to the whole world.

The title "New Testament" is a traditional label for these books. It is a variant translation of the phrase, "new covenant," the final covenantal arrangement promised by God in Moses and the OT prophets. Jesus is presented in the New Testament as the initiator and eventual consummator of all new covenant blessings. The title "testament" was preferred in English partly because the word can also suggest an official declaration presented after one's departure. After Jesus' departure via His ascension, the Holy Spirit inspired the writings of these revelations forming the New Testament.

All New Testament writings are occasional pieces written to address some situation which had arisen. None of the writings are abstract treatises. The original audience of each writing had questions, problems, or needs which the authors had in mind as they wrote. The purposes and occasions behind each of the NT writings will be addressed as they are presented throughout the work.

The arrangement of NT books in modern Bibles is not original and has varied over the millennia (see charts 69–71), but the order follows a logic which is nonetheless helpful. The first five books are historical writings: Gospels and Acts. The Gospels (Matthew, Mark, Luke, and John) recount the sayings and deeds of the Lord Jesus in the days of His earthly ministry. The book of Acts is a complement to Luke's Gospel, detailing how the message spread throughout Israel and the gentile world after the passion and ascension of Jesus.

The next collection of writings are the epistles, letters written by certain apostles and other prophetic leaders in the first century church. These writings address believers in different parts of the Roman empire facing various problems in their doctrine or practice. They flesh out what trusting and following Jesus meant for believers who had never seen Him in his earthly ministry. The first batch of epistles (Romans–Philemon), written by the Apostle Paul, have been arranged mostly in order of their length, and they have been named after their recipients. Paul's letters to churches are presented first followed by his letters to individual church leaders. The remaining epistles (Hebrews–Jude) were written by other apostles or prophets. With the exception the anonymous letter to the Hebrews, all of the letters have been named after their authors, not their recipients.

The final book in the New Testament is the Revelation, a transcription of visions given to the Apostle John late in his life near the end of the first century. These visions contain the last words of the ascended Lord Jesus and prophetic foretellings of the coming tribulation and glories around the Second Coming of the Lord.

All combined, these 27 New Testament writings provide the indispensable deposit of God's final written revelation centered around God's Son, the Living Word, and the believer's responsibility in light of such truth.

THE GOSPELS

The four Gospels recount the deeds and teachings of the Lord Jesus Christ, the Son of God. The fact that there are four extended records of Jesus' life indicates the magnitude of His importance in redemptive history. Throughout the Old Testament, some great events are recounted more than once. The creation account is told twice with different emphases (Gen 1 and 2) as are the histories of Israel and Judah in the books of Samuel, Kings, and Chronicles. The fall of Jerusalem in 586 BC is recounted in three books (Kings, Chronicles, and Isaiah). But there is nothing in the Bible rivaling the four-fold recounting of the life and ministry of the Christ.

Each Gospel is a biography of sorts about Jesus, highlighting the most important and memorable aspects of His life. The writers were either eyewitnesses to Jesus' life (Matthew and John) or associates of those who were (Mark and Luke). Each wrote to an audience in a region of their influence. Matthew wrote his Gospel to Jewish readers in Syria where he had settled in the mid-first century. Mark wrote about Jesus to residents in Rome where he had been ministering with Peter in the 50s or 60s. Luke wrote around the late 50's to a Greek individual named Theophilus, probably a convert of Paul's mission campaigns. John wrote to Jewish readers in the region of Ephesus where he settled in the latter portion of his ministry in the 70s–90s.

These four evangelists had specific reasons for writing their Spirit-inspired versions of the greatest story ever told. Matthew wrote to assure Jewish readers that Jesus was in fact the promised King of Israel. Mark wrote to show Romans that Jesus was the ultimate servant, a heroic man of action worthy of worship, faith, and obedience. Luke wrote to a Greek of high stature to assure him that Jesus was the Savior not only of the Jews but also the whole world. John wrote to Jews in the dispersion to persuade them that Jesus was the Son of the Living God. These themes are found throughout all four Gospels, but each book tends to emphasize one of these more than the others.

Technically, all of the Gospels are anonymous because the authors never identify themselves as such in the books. But their names were clearly associated with these works in the very early church, and details within the writings provide confirming evidence of these ancient associations.

While the Gospels are not carbon copies, they very often mirror each other in wording and details. The apostles' early preaching no doubt had a common way of recounting these stories long before any of them ever wrote a Gospel (the first written Gospel may not have been composed until a decade or two after Jesus' ascension). The variations in the stories and sayings of Jesus may be reckoned as alternative renderings of Jesus' original words (sometimes spoken in Aramaic but always written in Greek), or as faithful editing of the material for emphasis. Sometimes a Gospel recounts events from Jesus' life in a more topical way than in strict chronological order. Mark's Gospel is generally regarded as the most chronological. The Gospel of John is the most unique of all, written decades later than the others with the purpose of filling in the gaps of the other three. While the Gospels generally cover the whole of Jesus' life, they each give special attention to His passion. This demonstrates the centrality to the Christian message of Christ's work on the cross and His resurrection.

Matthew's Passion	Mark's Passion	Luke's Passion	John's Passion
15% of the book (7 chaps. out of 28)	40% of the book (5 chaps. out of 16)	24% of the book (4 long chaps. out of 24)	40% of the book (7.5 chaps. out of 21)

THE GOSPEL OF MATTHEW

The Gospel according to Matthew recounts the stories and teachings of Jesus from the perspective of Matthew, one of the Twelve apostles. Matthew's Hebrew name was "Levi," like the ancestral head of Israel's ministerial tribe. His more common name, "Matthew," is a nickname meaning, "Gift of God." Traditionally, Matthew was regarded as the first Gospel writer. Modern scholarship typically favors Mark as written first, assuming that Matthew's account is an enlargement of a shorter work. There is no need to assume, though, that Matthew, an eyewitness, needed to rely on a writing from a non-eyewitness.

Technically, the book is anonymous as the book nowhere directly lists Matthew as its author. But ancient Christian tradition (early AD 100's) associates the work with him, and there are several internal supporting indicators of this claim. Matthew was a tax collector by trade, a fact that only he unreservedly recounts (9:9). The other Gospels mildly obscure his shameful past by referring to him as "Levi" in those stories (Mark 2:14; Luke 5:27). Also, when the book tells of Jesus coming to his house (Matt 9:10), only Matthew's account refers to the domicile as "the house" whereas the other Gospels simply call it, "his house."

Matthew wrote his account for a Jewish audience in the mid-first century AD. Church tradition places him in the region of Syria at the time, ministering to Jewish converts. His concern for Jewish readers is underscored by several internal features: the book includes a Hebrew genealogy, references throughout of Jewish locations and customs with little explanation, various untranslated Aramaic words, and nearly three dozen quotations from the Old Testament. His burden is to assure his Jewish readers that Jesus Christ is in fact the promised King of Israel. In his recounting of Jesus' life, Matthew includes around 50 references to God's kingdom and eight references to Jesus as king. Ironically, the characters in the Gospel who most directly speak of Jesus' kingship are Gentiles—the Magi (2:2) and Pontius Pilate (27:11, 37). Near the middle of the book (chap. 11–13), the Jewish officials' rejection of Jesus' kingship represents a major turning point. From then on Jesus no longer spoke of the kingdom being "at hand."

Debate exists in Matthean studies concerning the structure of the book. Some follow a basic geographical movement of Jesus' starting in Judea (1:1–4:11) and ending in Jerusalem (21:1–28:20). Others emphasize the twice recurring phrase "from that time" (4:17; 16:21) as marking a focus on Jesus' origins, His ministry, and His passion. Still others favor a more complex approach viewing the book as structured as a large-scale chiasm where the book expands and retracts with corresponding details. The approach taken in VOCNT, however, is based on the book's pairing of narratives and discourses. The book alternates between collections of stories followed by Jesus' sermons, each followed by the phrase, "When Jesus had finished" (note the "Transition" at the bottom of each major column in Chart 1).

Scholars also debate whether Matthew intended his work to be evangelistic and apologetic (appealing to unbelieving Jews) or instructional and reaffirming (aimed at believing Jews). The high amount of Jesus' ethical teaching included in the book may tip the scale in favor of a believing audience, but one cannot dismiss evangelistic intent as well. Matthew's account could be called, "the Gospel of the Kingdom," as his desire is for his readers to be loyal and ready followers of the King.

The book ends with Jesus' famous "Great Commission" as He sends His disciples into the world to disciple the nations until His return and the consummation of His glorious kingdom.

CHART 1 **Matthew** ©2015 M. Scott Bashoor	***Purpose***: Matthew presents Jesus as the promised Messiah and King of Israel who, despite their rejection, will establish His long-promised kingdom. In each main section, Matthew alternates between narratives of Jesus' ministry and major discourses.	***Date:*** c. AD 50–65 ***Recipients:*** Christian Jews in Syria ***Author:*** Matthew, aka Levi

INTRODUCTION: **THE KING'S BIRTH & MIRACULOUS ARRIVAL FROM HEAVEN** **1:1–2:23**	**MAIN BODY:** **THE KING'S MIRACULOUS MINISTRY AND FIVE MAIN DISCOURSES** **3:1–26:2**					**CONCLUSION:** **THE KING'S DEATH, VICTORIOUS RESURRECTION & COMMISSION** **26:3–28:20**
	THE KING FORMALLY INTRODUCED TO ISRAEL **3:1–7:29**	**THE KING'S AUTHORITY POWERFULLY DISPLAYED** **8:1–11:1**	**THE KING'S AUTHORITY INCREASINGLY OPPOSED** **11:2–13:53**	**THE KING'S WITHDRAWAL & NEW PREPARATIONS** **13:54–19:2**	**THE KING OFFICIALLY REJECTED BY ISRAEL** **19:3–26:2**	
His Royal Genealogy **1:1–17** **The Angelic Explanation of the Virgin Birth** **1:18–25** **The Star-Signaled Arrival of the King of the Jews** **2:1–12** **The Flight of Safety to Egypt & the Fulfillment of Scripture** **2:13–23**	**NARRATIVES:** **Jesus' Entry into Public Ministry** **3:1–4:25** John the Baptist's Preparatory Ministry 3:1–17 Jesus' Wilderness Testing 4:1–11 Jesus' Early Ministry 4:12–25 **FIRST DISCOURSE:** **The Sermon on the Mt** **5:1–7:29** The Beatitudes 5:1–16 Amplification of the Law 5:17–48 Outworking of Righteousness 6:1–7:12 The Call to Decision 7:13–27 Transition 7:28–29	**NARRATIVES:** **Authentication thru His Many Miracles** **8:1–10:4** Healing Israel's Outcasts 8:1–17 Authority Over Disciples, Disease & Demons 8:16–9:17 Healing & Early Opposition 9:16–10:4 **SECOND DISCOURSE:** **The Kingdom Commissioning** **10:5–11:1** Short-Term Mission to Israel 10:5–15 Long-Term Anticipation of a Global Mission 10:16–23 The Marks of Disciples 10:24–10:42 Transition 11:1	**NARRATIVES:** **Stories of Mounting Opposition to Jesus** **11:2–12:50** Concern from John's Disciples 11:2–19 Unresponsive Cities & the Continuing Call 11:20–30 Conflict with Pharisees 12:1–45 Concern from Jesus' Family 12:46–50 **THIRD DISCOURSE:** **Parables of the Kingdom** **13:1–53** Parables of the Kingdom Told to the Crowds 13:1–35 Further Teaching Shared with the Disciples 13:36–52 Transition 13:53	**NARRATIVES:** **Conflicts & Crises Amidst Ministry in the North** **13:54–17:27** Cycles of Conflict & Continued Miraculous Authentication 13:54–16:20 The Defective Disciples & Their Need to be Prepared for Jesus' Upcoming Death 16:21–17:27 **FOURTH DISCOURSE:** **Children of the Kingdom** **18:1–19:2** Becoming Like Children, Caring for God's Family 18:1–14 Confronting Sin & Forgiving Sinners in the Life of the Church 18:15–35 Transition 19:1–2	**NARRATIVES:** **Growing Controversy Over Jesus' Teachings & Actions** **19:3–23:29** Controversy on the Way to Jerusalem 19:3–20:34 Controversy Upon Arrival in Jerusalem 21:1–23:39 **FIFTH DISCOURSE:** **The Olivet Discourse** **24:1–26:2** Coming Judgment & the Coming Kingdom 24:1–31 The Call to Readiness for His Coming 24:32–25:30 The King on His Throne of Judgment 25:31–46 Transition 26:1–2	**The Enemies' Plot & Jesus' Preparations** **26:3–35** **Withdrawal to Gethsemane & Arrest** **26:36–56** **The Trials of the Messiah** **26:57–27:26** **Jesus' Crucifixion & Burial** **27:27–66** **The Empty Tomb & the Resurrection** **28:1–15** **The Great Commission & the Ascension** **28:16–20**

CHART 2: Focus on Matthew 1:1–7:29

INTRODUCTION: The King's Birth & Miraculous Arrival from Heaven, 1:1–2:23

His Royal Genealogy 1:1–17

Introduction to Jesus' Lineage 1:1

Three Genealogical Cycles from Abraham to David to the Exile to Jesus 1:1–16

Symbolic Summary 1:17

Angelic Explanation of the Virgin Birth 1:18–25

The Star-Signaled Arrival of the King of the Jews 2:1–12

The Arrival of the Magi in Jerusalem in Search of the Newborn King 2:1–2

The Jealous Inquiry of Herod the Great 2:3–8

The Magi's Visit of Baby Jesus 2:9–12

The Flight of Safety to Egypt & the Fulfillment of Scripture 2:13–23

The Angelic Warning to Flee to Egypt & Jesus' Typological Fulfillment 2:13–15

Herod's Slaughter of the Innocents 2:16–18

The Angelic Call to Return to Judah 2:19–23

MAIN BODY: The King's Miraculous Ministry and Five Main Discourses, 3:1–26:2

The King Formally Introduced to Israel, 3:1–7:29

NARRATIVES: Jesus' Entry into Public Ministry 3:1–4:25

John the Baptist's Preparatory Ministry 3:1–17

John's Preaching of Repentance in the Wilderness in Advance of the Kingdom 3:1–12

John's Baptism of Jesus & the Divine Acclamation 3:13–17

Jesus' Wilderness Testing 4:1–11

Tempted to Selfishly Use Power 4:1–4

Tempted to Foolishly Test God 4:5–7

Tempted to Illicitly Gain Glory 4:8–11

Jesus' Early Ministry 4:12–25

His Move to Galilee after John's Imprisonment 4:12–17

His Quick Command of Disciples 4:18–22

Great Notoriety & Crowds for His Teaching & Healing Ministry 4:23–25

FIRST DISCOURSE: The Sermon on the Mount—Requirements for Life in the Kingdom 5:1–7:29

The Beatitudes 5:1–16

Introduction 5:1–2

Kingdom Blessings on the Righteous 5:3–12

The Call to be Salt & Light in the World 5:13–16

Amplification of the Law 5:17–48

His Fulfillment of the Law 5:17–20

Correction of Common Misperceptions of the Law 5:21–48

Regarding Murder 5:21–26

Regarding Adultery 5:27–30

Regarding Divorce 5:31–32

Regarding Oaths 5:33–37

Regarding Vengeance 5:38–42

Regarding Love & Hate 5:43–47

Concluding Call to Perfection 5:48

Outworking of Righteousness 6:1–7:12

Avoiding Hypocrisy 6:1–18

Introduction 6:1

Give Discreetly 6:2–4

Pray Privately & Thoughtfully 6:5–15

Fast Secretly 6:16–18

Storing Up Heavenly Treasure 6:19–24

Living by Faith, Not Anxiously 6:25–34

Forsaking Judgmentalism 7:1–6

Trusting God in Prayer & Imitating His Love 7:7–12

The Call to Decision 7:13–27

Enter the Narrow Gate 7:13–15

The True & False Known by Their Fruits 7:16–20

Warning of Final Judgment on False Followers 7:21–23

Foundations of Rock or Sand 7:24–27

Transition, 7:28–29

The King's Authority Powerfully Displayed, 8:1–11:1

The King's Authority Increasingly Opposed, 11:2–13:53

The King's Withdrawal & New Preparations, 13:54–19:2

The King Officially Rejected by Israel, 19:3–26:2

CONCLUSION, 26:3–28:20

CHART 3: Focus on Matthew 8:1–11:1

INTRODUCTION, 1:1–2:23

THE KING FORMALLY INTRODUCED TO ISRAEL, 3:1–7:29

MAIN BODY: THE KING'S MIRACULOUS MINISTRY AND FIVE MAIN DISCOURSES, 3:1–26:2

THE KING'S AUTHORITY POWERFULLY DISPLAYED, 8:1–11:1

NARRATIVES: Authentication thru His Many Miracles 8:1–10:4			SECOND DISCOURSE: The Kingdom Commissioning—Instructions for Messengers of the Kingdom 10:5–11:1			
Healing Israel's Outcasts 8:1–17	**Authority Over Disciples, Disease & Demons 8:16–9:9**	**Healing & Early Opposition 9:10–10:4**	**Short-Term Mission to Israel 10:5–15**	**Long-Term Anticipation of a Global Mission 10:16–23**	**The Marks of Disciples 10:24–42**	Transition, 11:1
A Leper Cleansed 8:1–4 The Centurion's Servant Raised Up 8:5–13 Peter's Mother-in-Law Healed 8:14–15 Many Sick & Demon-Possessed Delivered 8:16–17	Commanding Call to Discipleship (a Scribe) 8:16–22 Command Over the Sea 8:23–27 Command Over Demons in Gadara 8:28–34 Command Over Sickness & Sin 9:1–8 Commanding Call to Discipleship (Matthew) 9:9	Opposition Over His Outreach to Sinners 9:10–13 Opposition Over His Lack of Fasting 9:14–17 Raising the Dead Daughter, Healing the Hemorrhaging Woman 9:18–26 Healing Two Blind Men 9:27–31 Delivering the Mute Demonian 9:32–33 Accusation of Demonic Collusion 9:34 Compassion on the Multitudes 9:35–38 The Summoning of the Twelve 10:1–4	A Mission to Jews, Not Gentiles 10:5–6 The Message of the Nearness of the Kingdom 10:7 Attesting Miracles to Perform 10:8 Hospitality as the Means of Financial Support 10:9–11 Blessings & Curses Pronounced Based on Reception 10:12–15	Fierce Opposition as the Mission Extends to the Gentiles 10:16–18 The Promise of Divine Help to Testify Under Trial 10:19–20 Persecution to Continue until the End 10:21–23	Those Who Fear God, Not Men, & Trust in His Care 10:24–31 Those Who Confess Christ Before Hostile Men 10:32–33 Those Who Love Christ Even More Than Family 10:34–37 Those Who Take Up Their Cross to Follow Jesus 10:38–39 Those Who Receive God's Reward for Receiving Christ, His Message & His Messengers 10:40–42	

THE KING'S AUTHORITY INCREASINGLY OPPOSED, 11:2–13:53

THE KING'S WITHDRAWAL & NEW PREPARATIONS, 13:54–19:2

THE KING OFFICIALLY REJECTED BY ISRAEL, 19:3–26:2

CONCLUSION, 26:3–28:20

CHART 4: Focus on Matthew 11:2–13:53

INTRODUCTION, 1:1–2:23

MAIN BODY: THE KING'S MIRACULOUS MINISTRY AND FIVE MAIN DISCOURSES, 3:1–26:2

THE KING FORMALLY INTRODUCED TO ISRAEL, 3:1–7:29

THE KING'S AUTHORITY POWERFULLY DISPLAYED, 8:1–11:1

THE KING'S AUTHORITY INCREASINGLY OPPOSED, 11:2–13:53

NARRATIVES: Stories of Mounting Opposition to Jesus 11:2–12:50				THIRD DISCOURSE: Parables of the Kingdom—The Mystery Form of the Kingdom 13:1–53		
Concern from John's Disciples 11:2–19	**Unresponsive Cities & the Continuing Call to Repent 11:20–30**	**Conflict with the Pharisees 12:1–45**	**Concern from Jesus' Family 12:46–50**	**Parables of the Kingdom Told to the Crowds 13:1–35**	**Further Teaching Shared with the Disciples 13:36–52**	**Transition, 13:53**
John's Seeming Uncertainty about Jesus' Identity 11:2–3 Jesus' Assurance of His Attesting Works & Fulfillment of Scripture 11:4–6 Jesus' Commendation of John the Baptist 11:7–15 Indictment of the Jews for Rejecting John 11:16–19	Denunciations of Chorazin, Bethsaida & Capernaum for Not Repenting 11:20–24 Jesus' Prayer of Thanks for Calling the Humble 11:25–27 Jesus' Call to the Needy to Find Rest in Him 11:28–30	Conflict Over the Sabbath 12:1–21 *The Disciples Accused 12:1–2* *Jesus' Response from OT Precedent 12:3–8* *Jesus' Defense of Healing on the Sabbath 12:9–13* *The Pharisee's Rejection a Typical Fulfillment of Prophecy 12:14–21* Conflict Over Exorcism 12:22–45 *Accusation of Demonic Collusion 12:22–24* *Exorcism as a Sign of the Kingdom 12:25–29* *The Unpardonable Sin 12:30–32* *Pharisees, a Brood of Vipers 12:33–37* *The Demand for Another Sign 12:38–42* *The Rejecters Like Those Demonically Possessed 12:43–45*	His Mother & Brothers Seek an Intervention 12:46–47 Jesus' Declares Disciples to be His True Family 12:48–50	The Setting by the Sea 13:1–2 Parable of the Seed & Soils 13:3–23 *The Parable Declared 13:3–9* *Excursus: Jesus' Reason for Preaching in Parables—Concealment 13:10–17* *The Parable Explained 13:18–23* Parable of the Tares & Wheat 13:24–30 Parable of the Mustard Seed 13:31–32 Parable of the Hidden Leaven 13:33–35	The Setting in the House 13:36 Explanation of the Parable of the Tares & Wheat 13:37–43 Parable of the Hidden Treasure 13:44 Parable of the Pearl of Great Price 13:45–46 Parable of the Dragnet 13:47–50 Concluding Parable of Treasures New & Old 13:51–52	

THE KING'S WITHDRAWAL & NEW PREPARATIONS, 13:54–19:2

THE KING OFFICIALLY REJECTED BY ISRAEL, 19:3–26:2

CONCLUSION, 26:3–28:20

CHART 5: Focus on Matthew 13:54–19:2

INTRODUCTION, 1:1–2:23

MAIN BODY: THE KING'S MIRACULOUS MINISTRY AND FIVE MAIN DISCOURSES, 3:1–26:2

THE KING FORMALLY INTRODUCED TO ISRAEL, 3:1–7:29

THE KING'S AUTHORITY POWERFULLY DISPLAYED, 8:1–11:1

THE KING'S AUTHORITY INCREASINGLY OPPOSED, 11:2–13:53

THE KING'S WITHDRAWAL & NEW PREPARATIONS, 13:54–19:2

NARRATIVES: Conflicts & Crises Amidst Ministry in the North 13:54–17:27		FOURTH DISCOURSE: Children of the Kingdom—Greatness in the Kingdom 18:1–19:2		
Cycles of Conflict & Continued Miraculous Authentication 13:54–16:20	**The Defective Disciples & Their Need to be Prepared for Jesus' Upcoming Death 16:5–17:27**	**Becoming Like Children, Caring for God's Children 18:1–14**	**Confronting Sin & Forgiving Sinners in the Church 18:15–35**	Transition, 19:1-2
Unbelief & Rejection in His Hometown 13:54–58	The Disciples' Dullness in Understanding the "Leaven of the Pharisees" 16:5–12	The Call to Child-Like Conversion 18:1–4	The Need for Confrontation of the Unrepentant 18:15–20	
The Martyrdom of John the Baptist 14:1–12	Peter's Great Confession & Mistake 16:13–23	Spiritual Care for God's Children in Christ's Community 18:5–6	*Confrontation of Sin & the Practice of Church Discipline 18:15–17*	
The Feeding of the Five Thousand 14:13–21	*Peter Praised for Knowing Christ's Identity as Son of God 16:13–20*	The Removal of Stumbling Blocks of Sin 18:7–10 [11]	*Heavenly Authorization for Difficult Discipline 18:18–20*	
Jesus Walks on Water 14:22–33	*Peter Rebuked for Forbidding Jesus' Mission to the Cross 16:21–23*	*Stumbling Blocks in One's Own Life 18:7–9*	The Unlimited Offer of Forgiveness to the Repentant 18:21–35	
Mass Healings Around Gennesaret 14:34–36	The Cost of Discipleship Explained 16:24–27	*Stumbling Blocks for Others 18:10 [–11]*	Peter's Question on the Limits of Forgiveness 18:21	
Conflict Over Ritual Washing 15:1–20	Jesus' Transfiguration & Peter's Foolish Proposal 16:28–17:8	The Missing Sheep & God's Pursuit of His Little Ones 18:12–14	Jesus' Parable of the Unforgiving Servant 18:22–34	
The Pharisee's Traditions Negating God's Commandments 15:1–9	The Resurrection Foretold & the Elijah Prophecy Explained 17:9–13		Jesus' Application of the Parable 18:35	
Jesus Clarifies the Nature of Spiritual Defilement 15:10–20	The Disciples' Inability to Deliver the Demoniac Son 17:14–21			
The Faith of the Canaanite Woman 15:21–28	Jesus Foretells His Passion More Fully 17:22–23			
Mass Healings Around Galilee 15:29–31	The Temple Tax Lesson: Jesus Teaches He & His People are Free from the Temple 17:24–27			
The Feeding of the Four Thousand 15:32–39				
The Pharisees Demand Another Sign 16:1–4				

THE KING OFFICIALLY REJECTED BY ISRAEL, 19:3–26:2

CONCLUSION, 26:3–28:20

CHART 6: Focus on Matthew 19:3–26:2

INTRODUCTION, 1:1–2:23

MAIN BODY: The King's Miraculous Ministry and Five Main Discourses, 3:1–26:2

The King Formally Introduced to Israel, 3:1–7:29

The King's Authority Powerfully Displayed, 8:1–11:1

The Kings Authority Increasingly Opposed, 11:2–13:53

The King's Withdrawal & New Preparations, 13:54–19:2

The King Officially Rejected by Israel, 19:3–26:2

NARRATIVES: Growing Controversy Over Jesus' Teachings & Actions 19:3–23:29

Controversy on the Way to Jerusalem 19:3–20:34

Controversy Over Divorce 19:3–12

Contention with Pharisees Over God's Law & God's Original Design 19:3–9

The Disciples' Discomfort; Jesus' Teaching on Kingdom Eunuchs 19:10–12

Correction about Children's Access 19:13–15

Lessons from the Rich Young Man 19:16–26

Controversial Teaching on Reward & the Parable of the Laborers 19:27–20:16

Peter's Claim of Sacrifice 19:27

Jesus' Teaching on Reward 19:28–30

The Parable of the Laborers 20:1–16

The Passion Foretold Again 20:17–19

The Disciples' Quest for Preference Rebuked 20:20–28

The Blind Men's Request for Mercy Granted 20:29–34

Controversy Upon Arrival in Jerusalem 21:1–23:39

The Triumphal Entry 21:1–11

The Cleansing of the Temple 21:12–17

Emblematic Curse of the Barren Fig Tree 21:18–22

Jesus' Authority Questioned 21:23–22:27

Parables Aimed at the Jewish Leaders 21:28–22:14

Parable of the Two Sons 21:27–32

Parable of the Wicked Tenants 21:33–44

Aside: Leader's Seek to Take Jesus 21:45–46

Parable of the Wedding Feast 22:1–14

Interchange of Trap Questions 22:15–46

Trap Question Over Tribute to Caesar 22:15–22

Trap Question on Marriage & Resurrection 22:23–33

Trap Question on the Commandments 22:34–40

Jesus' Trap Question on David's Son 22:41–46

Indictment of the Pharisees & Scribes 23:1–12

Eight Woes Against the Pharisees & Scribes 23:13–36

Jesus Weeps Over Jerusalem 23:37–39

FIFTH DISCOURSE: The Olivet Discourse–Revelation of Things to Come 24:1–26:2

Coming Judgment & the Coming Kingdom 24:1–31

The Temple Setting 24:1

The Temple's Overthrow Foretold 24:2

Prophecy of Other Future Events 24:3–31

Signs During This Age: The Beginning of Birth Pangs 24:3–14

Signs of the Great Tribulation to Come 24:15–28

Signs of the Glorious Return of Christ 24:29–31

The Call to Readiness for His Coming 24:32–25:30

Parable of the Ripe Fig Tree 24:32–35

The Hour Unknown 24:36

Many to be Unprepared as in Noah's Day 24:37–41

The Command to Be Ready to Give Account 24:42–51

Parable of the Ten Virgins 25:1–13

Parable of the Talents 24:14–30

The King on His Throne of Judgment 25:31–46

The Coming Separation of Sheep & Goats 25:31–33

Future Reception of the Righteous into the Kingdom 25:34–40

Future Dismissal of the Wicked to Everlasting Judgment 25:41–46

Transition, 26:1–2

CONCLUSION, 26:3–28:20

CHART 7: Focus on Matthew 26:3–28:20

INTRODUCTION, 1:1–2:23	MAIN BODY, 3:1–26:2					CONCLUSION: THE KING'S DEATH, VICTORIOUS RESURRECTION & COMMISSION, 26:3–28:20					
	THE KING FORMALLY INTRODUCED TO ISRAEL, 3:1–7:29	THE KING'S AUTHORITY POWERFULLY DISPLAYED, 8:1–11:1	THE KING'S AUTHORITY INCREASINGLY OPPOSED, 11:2–13:53	THE KING'S WITHDRAWAL & NEW PREPARATIONS, 13:54–19:2	THE KING OFFICIALLY REJECTED BY ISRAEL, 19:3–26:2	**The Enemies' Plot & Jesus' Preparations 26:3–35**	**Withdrawal to the Garden of Gethsemane & His Arrest 26:36–56**	**The Trials of the Messiah 26:57–27:26**	**Jesus' Crucifixion & Burial 27:27–66**	**The Empty Tomb & the Resurrection 28:1–15**	**The Great Commission 28:16–20**
						The Religious Leader's Plot Jesus' Downfall 26:3–5 Jesus Anointed in Bethany for His Burial 26:6–13 Judas Conspires to Betray Jesus 26:14–16 The Last Passover & Jesus Prophecy of His Betrayal 26:17–25 Institution of the Lord's Supper 26:26–30 Prophecy of Peter's Denial 26:31–35	Jesus Wrestles with God's Will in Prayer While the Disciples Slumber 26:36–46 Judas Arrives with Troops & Betrays Jesus with a Kiss 26:47–50 Jesus Disarms Conflict by Healing the Wounded Servant 26:51–56	The Trial Before Caiaphas 26:57–75 *The Initial Failure of the Kangaroo Court 26:57–60a* *The Charge of Temple Destruction 26:60b–62* *The Sentence of Blasphemy 26:63–68* *The "Side Trials" of Peter & Judas 26:69–27:10* *Peter's Failure to Testify in the Courtyard 26:69–75* Segue: The Extradition of Jesus to Pilate 27:1–2 Judas' Self-Sentencing & Suicide 27:3–10 The Trial Before Pilate 27:11–26 *Pilate's Puzzled Initial Evaluation 27:11–14* *The Offer to Release Barabbas or Jesus 27:15–18* *The Inspired Warning of Pilate's Wife 27:19* *The Insistence of the Jewish Leadership to Crucify Jesus 27:20–23* *Pilate's Capitulation, Barabbas' Release, Jesus' Consignment to Execution 27:24–26*	Jesus Beaten & Mockingly Acclaimed as King 27:27–31 The Crucifixion of the King on Golgotha 27:32–36 The Mockery of the Crowd & the Convicts 27:37–44 The Misunderstood Cry of Dereliction 27:45–49 Jesus' Death 27:50 Aftermath of His Death 27:51–54 *The Rending of the Temple Veil 27:51* *The Resurrection of Saints 27:52* *The Testimony of the Centurion 27:53* *The Remaining Witnesses 27:54–56* Jesus' Honorable Burial 27:57–66 *The Securing of Jesus' Body & Donation of Joseph's Tomb 27:54–61* *The Conspirators Seal the Tomb to Prevent a Resurrection Conspiracy 27:62–66*	The Angelic Explanation to the Two Marys About the Empty Tomb 28:1–7 The Resurrected Jesus Greets the Women & Commissions Them to Tell the Disciples 28:8–10 The Chief Priest's Conspiracy to Explain the Empty Tomb as a Theft 28:11–15	The Setting in Galilee 28:16 The Hesitance of the Worshipping Disciples 28:17 The Commission to Make Disciples Until the End of the Age 28:18–20

THE GOSPEL OF MARK

The shortest of the four Gospels was penned around AD 64–68 by John Mark. The book is titled after his Latin name which is appropriate since he wrote for Roman readers (Acts 12:25). Mark wrote his Gospel to set forth God's Son as the ultimate servant and a man of action who came to redeem the world (Mark 10:45).

Mark's gospel reflects the preaching of Peter with whom he was ministering in Rome before Peter's martyrdom (1 Pet 5:13). The early church father Papias (AD 70–155) described Mark as "Peter's interpreter," one who wrote down Peter's memoirs. Unsurprisingly, Peter has a more prominent role in this Gospel than the others.

Mark was probably a young man in Jerusalem during Jesus' ministry, and he may have been present for the passion. His family might have owned the upper room (Acts 12:12), and perhaps he is the unnamed young man who escapes the scene of Jesus' arrest—a curious note mentioned only by him (14:51–52). What's known for certain is that he was closely connected to the early church being Barnabas's cousin (Col 4:10) and an associate of Paul and Peter.

Numerous features in Mark's Gospel would appeal to a Roman audience. For instance, Mark includes no genealogy of Jesus; Roman audiences were typically uninterested in such things. Instead, Mark spends most of his efforts telling the stories of Jesus in a rapid-fire manner that Romans would appreciate, often stringing them together with the word, "immediately." Mark also explains unfamiliar Jewish customs and translates Aramaic words for his Gentile audience to help bridge the gap of their understanding.

While Mark doesn't include Jesus' more lengthy teachings, the ones he features tend to focus on the nature of discipleship. In the center of the book is found Jesus' famous line, "If anyone wishes to come after Me, he must deny himself, and take up his cross and follow Me" (8:34). By favoring these words of Jesus, Mark reveals his desire to reach Romans and see them become followers of Jesus by faith.

The structure of Mark follows the major geographical movements of Jesus. The introduction (1:1–13) highlights the preparatory work by John the Baptist in Judea. The first half of the book (1:14–8:30) traces Jesus' ministry in northern Israel. In His early ministry there, Jesus announces the arrival of the kingdom. As He puts his authority on display, His ministry reaches an exciting climax as Jews and Gentiles believe in Him. But in the second half of the book (8:31–15:41), Jesus begins moving toward Jerusalem for what will be a showdown with the local authorities. The more Jesus directly reveals His identity, the more opposition He faces until His claim as Son of God is utterly and unjustly rejected. God then vindicates his Son in the resurrection (15:42ff), and the short ending of the book leaves the reader shocked over the good news of His victory.

Part of the drama of Mark's account is that the divine identity of Jesus is gradually revealed in the stories (though it is asserted directly in the opening verse). By the end of the story, there's no doubt that Jesus is who the Roman centurion declared Him to be: "Truly, this man was the Son of God" (15:39).

CHART 8 **Mark** ©2015 M. Scott Bashoor	***Purpose:*** Mark presents Jesus as God's Son and anointed Savior, a Man of action who came to redeem the world. Roman Christians would be encouraged to continue following Jesus after reading how His identity was disclosed in His ministry.	***Date:*** *c.* AD 64–68 ***Recipients:*** Gentile Roman Believers ***Author:*** Mark, Recounting Peter's Teaching

INTRODUCTION: **The Greatness of Jesus Christ Attested from the Beginning** **1:1–13**	**MAIN BODY:** **The Disclosure of God's Son & Anointed Savior of the World** **1:13–15:47**						**CONCLUSION:** **The Greatness of Jesus Christ Attested in Resurrection** **15:42–16:8** **[9–20]**
	Jesus' Ministry in the North: **Jesus' Identity Revealed in Measure** **1:14–8:30**			**Jesus' Ministry Moves To Jerusalem: The Son of God Fully Revealed & Finally Rejected** **8:31–15:41**			
Title **1:1** **Prologue: The Greatness of Jesus Christ** **1:2–13**	**Early Ministry in Galilee: Announcement of the Kingdom** **1:14–3:6**	**Climax of the Galilean Ministry: Authority on Display** **3:7–6:6a**	**The Ministry Expands: Gentiles & Jews Believe** **6:6b–8:30**	**Move Toward Jerusalem: The Passion Foretold** **8:31–10:52**	**Ministry Around & In Jerusalem: Welcome & Rejection** **11:1–13:37**	**The Passion of the Lord: Shame & Honor Received** **14:1–15:41**	**The Honorable Burial of Jesus** **15:42–47** **The Resurrection** **16:1–8**
Attested by John the Baptist in the Wilderness 1:2–8 *John's Ministry a Fulfillment of Prophecies* *1:2–3* *John's Preaching of Repentance* *1:4–6* *John's Preparation for Christ* *1:7–8* Attested by God at Jesus' Baptism 1:9–11 Proven in Satan's Temptation in the Wilderness 1:12–13	Intro. Sketch 1:14–15 The First Disciples Called 1:16–20 Miraculous Power Over Sickness & Demons 1:21–45 Five Conflicts with Religious Leaders 2:1–3:5 Concluding Rejection by Pharisees & Herodians 3:6	Intro. Sketch 3:7–12 The Calling of the Twelve 3:13–19 Conflicts in Capernaum 3:20–35 Kingdom Parables 4:1–34 Attesting Miracles in Decapolis & Galilee 4:35–5:43 Concluding Rejection at Nazareth 6:1–6a	Intro. Sketch 6:6b The 12 Sent Amid Hostility 6:7–32 More Miracles in Galilee 6:33–56 Conflict with the Pharisees 7:1–23 More Miracles & Spiritual Blindness 7:24–8:26 Concluding Confession by Peter 8:27–30	First Prophecy on the Passion Unit: *The Disciples' Deficiencies Exposed* 8:31–9:29 Second Prophecy on the Passion Unit: *True Discipleship Explained* 9:30–10:31 Third Prophecy on the Passion Unit: *The Disciple's Humility Encouraged* 10:32–45 Concluding Confession & Healing of Bartimaeus 10:46–52	The Triumphal Entry into Jerusalem: *Welcomed by the Pilgrims* 11:1–10 Climactic Conflict with the Temple: *Rejected by the Establishment* 11:11–12:44 The Olivet Discourse: *The Judgment & Kingdom to Come* 13:1–37	The Enemies' Plot & Jesus' Preparations 14:1–52 The Jewish & Roman Trials 14:53–15:15 The Crucifixion 15:16–37 Concluding Confirmations & Confession 15:38–41	The Empty Tomb Found & Explained 16:1–7 The Concluding Shock of the Good News 16:8 **[Appendix: "The Long Ending"** **16:9–20]** Jesus Seen by Mary Magdalene & the Two on the Road [16:9–12] The Eleven Commissioned [16:13–18] The Ascension & Commencement of the Mission [16:19–20]

CHART 9: Focus on Mark 1:14–6:6a

INTRODUCTION, 1:1–13

MAIN BODY: THE DISCLOSURE OF GOD'S SON & ANOINTED SAVIOR OF THE WORLD, 1:14–15:47

JESUS' MINISTRY IN THE NORTH: JESUS' IDENTITY REVEALED IN MEASURE, 1:14–8:30

Jesus' Early Ministry in Galilee: Announcement of the Kingdom 1:14–3:6				Climax of the Galilean Ministry: Authority on Display 3:7–6:6a				
Intro-ductory Sketch	**Miraculous Power Over Sickness & Demons 1:21–45**	**Five Conflicts with Religious Leaders 2:1–3:5**	**Concluding Rejection by the Pharisees & Herodians, 3:6**	**Introductory Sketch 3:7–12**	**Conflicts in Capernaum 3:20–35**	**Kingdom Parables 4:1–34**	**Attesting Miracles in Decapolis & Galilee 4:35–5:43**	**Con-cluding Rejec-tion at Nazareth 6:1–6a**
Jesus Preaches the Kingdom & Repent-ance **1:14–15** **The First Disciples Called** Simon, Andrew, James & John **1:16–20**	Synagogue Teaching Confirmed by Exorcism 1:21–28 Healings & Exorcisms in Caper-naum: Peter's Mother-in-Law & the Masses 1:29–34 Strategic Ministry Withdrawal to Other Towns 1:35–39 Cleansing the Leper & Insisting on His Silence 1:40–45	The Healing of the Paralytic & Jesus' Authority to Forgive Sins 2:1–12 The Calling of Levi & Jesus' Association with Sinners 2:13–17 Jesus' Lack of Fasting: The Bridegroom is Present 2:18–22 Grain-Plucking on Sabbath: Jesus is Lord of the Sabbath 2:23–28 The Healing of the Shriveled Hand: Jesus is Lord of the Sabbath 3:1–5		Growing Crowds from throughout the Land 3:7–8 Maneuvering to Minister to Multitudes 3:9–10 Testimony of Demons Wisely Silenced 3:11–12 **Calling of the Twelve 3:13–19** The Mountain Setting 3:13 Investiture of Authority 3:14–15 The List 3:16–19	Jesus' Family Wrongly Concerned 3:20–21 The Pharisee's Accusation of Satanic Collusion: The Unpardon-able Sin 3:22–30 Jesus' Family's Misguided Concern& Jesus' True Spiritual Family 3:31–35	Parable of the Sower & the Soils 4:1–9 The Purpose of Parables Explained to the Twelve 4:10–12 Explanation of the Sower & the Soils 4:13–20 Parable of the Lamp & Its Application 4:21–25 Parable of the Seed 4:26–29 Parable of the Mustard Seed 4:30–34	The Stilling of the Sea 4:35–41 Exorcism of the Gerasene 5:1–20 *His Extreme Bondage 5:1–5* *The Demons' Recognition of Jesus 5:6–7* *The Demons Sent Away into the Swine 5:8–13* *Jesus Sent Away by the Herders 5:14–17* *The Delivered Man Sent Away to Testify in Decapolis 5:18–20* Two Miracles Involving Females & Twelves 5:21–43 *Request to Heal the Twelve-year-old Daughter 5:21–24* *Healing of the Twelve-year Hemorrhage 5:25–34* *Raising of the Twelve-year-old Daughter 5:35–43*	Return to His Home-town 6:1 Interest & Skepti-cism from the Syna-gogue 6:2–3 An Honor-able Prophet Deprived of Honor 6:4 Few Amazing Miracles Due to Amazing Unbelief 6:5–6a

The Ministry Expands: Gentiles & Jews Believe, 6:6b–8:30

JESUS' MINISTRY MOVES TO JERUSALEM: THE SON OF GOD FULLY REVEALED & FINALLY REJECTED, 8:31–15:41

CONCLUSION, 15:42–16:8 [20]

CHART 10: Focus on Mark 6:6b–10:52

Introduction, 1:1–13	Main Body: The Disclosure of God's Son & Anointed Savior of the World, 1:14–15:47												Conclusion, 15:42–16:8 [20]
	Jesus' Ministry in the North: Jesus' Identity Revealed in Measure 1:14–8:30						Jesus' Ministry Moves To Jerusalem: The Son of God Fully Revealed & Finally Rejected 8:31–15:41						
	The Ministry Expands: Gentiles & Jews Believe 6:6b–8:30						Move Toward Jerusalem: The Passion Foretold 8:31–10:52				Ministry Around & In Jerusalem: Welcome & Rejection, 11:1–13:37	The Passion of the Lord: Shame & Honor Received, 14:1–15:41	
	Introductory Sketch: Jesus Preaching in the Villages, 6:6b	**The Twelve Sent Amid Hostility 6:7–32** Short-Term Mission of the Twelve 6:7–13 The Climate of Persecution 6:14–29 *Herod's Anxiety 6:14–16* *Retrospect on Herod's Execution of John for Confronting His Immorality 6:17–29* The Twelve Report Back to Jesus 5:30–32	**More Miracles in Galilee 6:33–56** Feeding of the 5,000: A Sign for the Masses 6:33–44 Walking on the Water: A Sign for the Twelve 6:45–52 Mass Healings in Gennesaret 6:53–55 Summary of Mass Healings in Galilee 6:56	**Conflict with the Pharisees 7:1–23** Controversy over Hand Washing 7:1–8 Indictment of Corban Traditions 7:9–13 Instruction on Spiritual Defilement 7:14–23 *The Lesson for the Crowd 7:14–16* *The Follow-up for the Dense Disciples 7:19–23*	**More Miracles & Spiritual Blindness 7:24–8:26** The Tyranese Daughter 7:24–30 The Deaf Man in the Northern Campaign 7:31–37 Feeding of the 4,000 8:1–10 The Blind Pharisees Demand another Sign 8:11–13 The Blind Disciples Seek Clarity 8:14–21 Two-Stage Healing of the Blind Man 8:22–26	**Concluding Confession by Peter 8:27–30** Jesus' Query on Popular Opinion of His Identity 8:27–28 Peter's Confession of Jesus as the Christ 8:29 The Command to Keep the Secret 8:30	**First Unit of Prophesy on the Passion: *The Disciples' Deficiencies Exposed* 8:31–9:29** Death & Resurrection to Come in Jerusalem 8:31–33 Call to Discipleship 8:34–38 Jesus' Transfiguration 9:1–8 Explanation of the Elijah Prophecy 9:9–13 Inability of Prayerless Disciples to Exorcise & Heal the Deaf-Mute Boy 9:14–29	**Second Unit of Prophesy on the Passion: *True Discipleship Explained* 9:30–10:31** Death & Resurrection to Come in Jerusalem 9:30–32 True Greatness in the Kingdom 9:33–50 *Servants of All 9:33–37* *Cooperation with Other Servants 9:38–41* *Care about Offenses in Light of Judgment 9:42–50* Teaching on Divorce 10:1–12 Welcoming of Children 10:13–16 The Rich Young Ruler & Eternal Rewards 10:17–31	**Third Unit of Prophesy on the Passion: *The Disciple's Humility Encouraged* 10:32–45** Death & Resurrection to Come in Jerusalem 10:32–34 Ambitions of James & John Corrected 10:35–40 Teaching on True Greatness 10:41–45 *Calming Instruction on Being Slaves of All 10:41–44* *The Son's Mission to Serve & Ransom 10:45*	**Concluding Confession & Healing of Bartimaeus 10:46–52** Setting: Leaving Jericho for Jerusalem 10:46 The Blind Man's Perception of Jesus' Identity 10:47–48 Jesus' Restoring His Sight & Commending His Faith 10:49–52			

CHART 11: Focus on Mark 11:1–15:41

INTRODUCTION, 1:1–13

MAIN BODY: THE DISCLOSURE OF GOD'S SON & ANOINTED SAVIOR OF THE WORLD, 1:14–15:47

JESUS' MINISTRY IN THE NORTH: JESUS' IDENTITY REVEALED IN MEASURE, 1:14–8:30

JESUS' MINISTRY MOVES TO JERUSALEM: THE SON OF GOD FULLY REVEALED & FINALLY REJECTED, 8:31–15:41

Move Toward Jerusalem: The Passion Foretold, 8:31–10:52

CONCLUSION, 15:42–16:8 [20]

Ministry Around & In Jerusalem: Welcome & Rejection 11:1–13:37			The Passion of the Lord: Shame & Honor Received 14:1–15:41			
Triumphal Entry into Jerusalem: *Welcomed by the Pilgrims* 11:1–10	**Climactic Conflict with the Temple: *Rejected by the Establishment* 11:11–12:44**	**The Olivet Discourse: *The Judgment & Kingdom to Come* 13:1–37**	**The Enemies' Plot & Jesus' Preparations 14:1–52**	**The Jewish & Roman Trials 14:53–15:15**	**The Crucifixion 15:16–37**	**Concluding Confirmations & Confession 15:38–41**
Arrangements Made for Pickup of a Donkey 11:1–7 Acclamation of Jesus' Kingship by the Pilgrim Crowds 11:8–10	Inspection of the Temple & Withdrawal to Bethany 11:11 Cursing of the Fig Tree & Cleansing of the Temple 11:12–25 [26] Dispute Over Jesus' Authority 11:27–33 Provocative Parable of the Wicked Tenant Famers 12:1–12 Trap Question on Roman Taxes 12:13–17 Trap Question on the Resurrection 12:18–27 Sincere Question on the Greatest Commandment 12:28–34 David's Son Greater than David 12:35–37 Indictment of the Scribes for Taking Advantage of Widows 12:38–40 Observation of the Poor Widow's Costly Donation 12:41–44	Private Instruction on the Temple's Destruction 13:1–4 Signs of the Current Age: Not the End 13:5–13 Signs of the End of the Age: The Abomination of Desolation 13:14–23 The Return of the Son & the Gathering of the Elect 13:24–27 The Coming Certain but the Time Unknown 13:28–37 *Parable of the Fig Tree & the Certainty of the Coming Change 13:28–32* *Concluding Call to Be Alert 13:33–37*	The Post-Passover Plot 14:1–2 The Pre-anointing of Jesus' Body for Burial 14:3–9 Judas' Betrayal to the Chief Priests 14:10–11 The Last Passover & Announcement of Betrayal 14:12–21 The Lord's Supper Instituted 14:22–26 Prophecy of the Disciples' Failure & Peter's Denial 14:27–31 The Agony & Arrest in Gethsemane 14:32–52 *Jesus Wrestles in Prayer as the Disciples Sleep 14:32–42* *Judas' Arrival with the Troops & Jesus' Arrest 14:43–52*	Jesus' Trial before the High Priest's Court 14:53–65 *Initial Failure to Prove Any Charges 14:53–59* *Conviction of Blasphemy for Identifying as God's Son 14:60–65* Peter's "Trial" & Denials in the Courtyard 14:66–72 Jesus' Trial in Pilate's Court 15:1–15 *Pilate Puzzled in His Initial Interrogation 15:1–5* *Pilate's Proposal to Release Jesus Instead of Barabbas 15:6–10* *Pilate's Expedient Decision to Execute Jesus 15:11–15*	The Abuse of the "King of the Jews" 15:16–20a The Procession to the Execution Site 15:20b–23 The Crucifixion of the King 15:24–26 Three Hours of Pain & Excessive Shame 15:27–32 Three Hours of Darkness 15:33 Jesus' Ninth Hour Cry of Dereliction & Its Misunderstanding 15:34–36 The Death of the King 15:37	Confirmation from Heaven: The Rending of the Temple Veil 15:38 Confession of the Centurion: A Roman's Recognition of God's Son 15:39 Confirmation of the Witnesses: The Women Remaining to the End 15:40–41

THE GOSPEL OF LUKE

Luke's Gospel was written near the time of Paul's journey to Rome somewhere around AD 59–61. Luke wrote his work to Theophilus, a wealthy Gentile convert and supporter of Paul's ministry who needed assurance that the gospel of the Jewish Messiah was for Gentiles also. Luke's Gospel is the first piece of this argumentation, continued later by the book of Acts. The two books are meant to be read together in complementary fashion.

Luke was not an eyewitness to Jesus' ministry but was a convert of the apostolic ministry. He began traveling with Paul on his second missionary journey (Acts 16:10). Luke acknowledged that his Gospel narrative is the result of research (Luke 1:3). He may well have been a Gentile and thus the only non-Jewish NT author. His sharp vocabulary and writing style coupled with his medical training (Col 4:4) suggests Luke was highly educated. When his Gospel is paired with Acts, Luke's writings are the lengthiest in all the New Testament, comprising 28% of the whole.

Luke's concern that the gospel message is also for Gentiles is evident in many places. He traces Jesus' heritage not only through David and Abraham but also Adam, showing He was the Man to redeem the whole human race. Luke is the only Gospel writer to recount well known parables such as the "Good Samaritan" (10:30–37) and the "Prodigal Son" (15:11–32), both of which are sympathetic to Gentile sensibilities. Throughout Luke's Gospel, Jesus is viewed as fulfilling Scripture and following the divine plan which must come to pass. While the Jewish rejection of Jesus ending in his crucifixion was tragic, this was part of the divine plan as well, fulfilling OT prophecies. One verse which highlights this overarching theme of God's plan is found near the beginning: "For my eyes have seen Your salvation which You have prepared in the presence of all peoples, A LIGHT OF REVELATION TO THE GENTILES, And the glory of Your people Israel" (Luke 2:30–32).

The grand structure of Luke has long been a matter of debate. While there is strong agreement on the individual units that make up the stories and sayings of Jesus, there is no general consensus on the larger structural flow. Many Roman numeral outlines of Luke include collections of 25 subsections or more, often conveniently stopping at the end of the English alphabet.

The structural approach charted on the next page sees the book beginning with a long introduction (1:1–4:13) which introduces Jesus against the backdrop of supernatural events preceding His public ministry. The body of the book follows the geographical movements of Jesus' ministry beginning in Galilee (4:14–9:50) as it is here where He calls the disciples, reveals Himself to the multitudes, and grows His core group of followers. In the second section, Jesus begins His move toward Jerusalem which Luke presents as a lengthy travel narrative (9:51–19:27). Three collections of stories and sermons show how Jesus instructed the disciples in their duties, formed their character, and prepared them for the difficult future. The final section focuses on His ministry in Jerusalem (19:28–21:38). His arrival and actions stir up controversy, and Jesus foretells the future fall of the Temple and the coming end of days.

The book ends with a long conclusion that brings Jesus' earthly ministry to its dramatic close (22:1–24:53). His passion and resurrection leave no doubt about God's sovereign plan, and the book ends with Jesus' promise to send the Spirit to continue His work.

CHART 12 Luke ©2015 M. Scott Bashoor	***Purpose:*** Luke writes a well-researched account for Theophilus about the ministry of Jesus Christ to reassure him that is was truly God's sovereign plan for Jesus to give himself as a sacrifice for the sins of the world (including Gentiles).		***Date:*** *c.* AD 58–60 ***Recipient:*** Theophilus (a Gentile convert of Paul?) ***Author:*** Luke, a ministry associate of Paul	
INTRODUCTION: EXTENSIVE PROLOGUE TO JESUS' EARTHLY MINISTRY 1:1–4:13	**MAIN BODY: THE REVELATION OF GOD'S SON & MAN'S SAVIOR THRU HIS MANY WORKS & WORDS 4:14–21:38**			**CONCLUSION: DRAMATIC CULMINATION TO JESUS' EARTHLY MINISTRY 22:1–24:53**
	JESUS' MINISTRY IN GALILEE: JESUS REVEALED AS SON OF GOD & MAN 4:14–9:50	**JESUS' MINISTRY ON THE WAY TO JERUSALEM: DISCIPLES PREPARED FOR JESUS' REJECTION 9:51–19:27**	**THE MINISTRY OF JESUS IN JERUSALEM: JESUS REJECTED & JERUSALEM DOOMED 19:28–21:38**	
The Author's Foreword 1:1–4 **Supernatural Preliminaries to Jesus' Ministry 1:5–4:13** The Miraculous Births of John the Baptist & Jesus 1:5–2:38 The Amazing Early Years of Jesus 2:39–52 John's Momentous Baptism of the Son of God 3:1–38 Satan's Failed Temptation of the Son of God 4:1–13	**The Beginning of the Ministry: Rejection, Relocation & Reception 4:14–44** **The Calling of the Disciples & Creation of a New Community 5:1–6:49** Calling Disciples, Curing Diseases & Commanding Authority 5:1–6:16 The Sermon on the Plain 6:17–49 **The Revelation of Jesus to the Multitudes 7:1–8:56** Questions of Jesus' Identity Answered 7:1–8:3 Cryptic Revelations in the Parables 8:4–21 Power Over the Natural & Supernatural 8:22–56 **The Disciples' Ministry Enlarged & Jesus' Mission Clarified 9:1–50** The Successful Mission of the Twelve 9:1–9 Jesus' Glory & the Path to Greatness 9:10–50	**Collection One from the Journey to Jerusalem: *Instructing the Disciples on Their Duties* 9:51–13:21** The Ministry Expanded in Samaria & by the Seventy 9:51–10:37 Samplings of Ministry in Bethany & Judea 10:38–13:21 **Collection Two from the Journey to Jerusalem: *Forming the Disciples in Their Character* 13:22–17:10** The Narrow Way, Oppositions & Invitations 13:22–14:24 Collection of Teachings to the Crowds, the Disciples & the Adversaries 14:25–17:10 **Collection Three from the Journey to Jerusalem: *Preparing the Disciples for The Future* 17:11–19:27** The Mercy of the King & the Coming Kingdom 17:11–18:8 Grace to the Humble & Reward for Service 18:9–18:30 The King's Coming Rejection, Saving Power, & the Delayed Kingdom 18:31–19:27	**Controversy Stirred in Jerusalem 19:28–21:4** The Triumphal Entry 19:28–40 Jesus' Lament Over Jerusalem 19:41–44 The Cleansing of the Temple 19:45–48 Controversies with the Religious Leadership 20:1–21:4 **The Olivet Discourse & the Temple's Destruction 21:5–38** The Future Fall of the Temple & The End Times 21:5–24 The Final Coming of the Son of Man 21:25–36 Transition 21:37–38	**The Passion of the Lord 22:1–23:56** The Enemies' Plot & Jesus' Preparations 22:1–46 The Arrest & Trials of Jesus 22:47–23:25 The Crucifixion & Burial of Jesus 23:26–56 **The Resurrection, Commission & Ascension 24:1–53** The Resurrection Announced & Confirmed 24:1–43 The Great Commission & the Lord's Ascension 24:44–53

CHART 13: Focus on Luke 1:1–4:13

INTRODUCTION: Extensive Prologue to Jesus' Earthly Ministry 1:1–4:13

Author's Foreword 1:1–4

- **Acknowledgment of Various Sources 1:1–3a**
- **Recipient of the Book: Theophilus 1:3b**
- **Purpose of the Book: To Engender Confidence in What Theophilus Had Already Been Taught 1:4**

Supernatural Preliminaries to Jesus' Ministry 1:4–4:13

The Miraculous Births of John the Baptist & Jesus 1:5–2:38

Their Births Foretold 1:5–38

- Announcement to Zechariah 1:5–25
  - *The Angelic Announcement to a Barren Family 1:5–17*
  - *Zechariah's Unbelief Silenced 1:18–25*
- Announcement to Mary 1:26–38
  - *Prophecy of Messiah's Birth to Mary 1:26–33*
  - *Explanation of the Virginal Conception 1:34–38*

Mary & Elizabeth Visit & Rejoice 1:39–56

- Account of Their Visit 1:39–45
- Mary's Magnificat 1:46–56

The Birth of John 1:57–80

- John's Birth Narrative 1:57–66
- Zechariah's Prophecy 1:67–79
- Summary of His Early Years 1:80

The Birth of Jesus 2:1–38

- Jesus' Birth Narrative 2:1–20
  - *The Roman Census & Move to Bethlehem for the Birth 2:1–7*
  - *The Announcement to the Shepherds & Their Arrival 2:8–20*
- Jesus' Presentation by His Parents in the Temple 2:21–38
  - *Protocols for the Poor Followed 2:21–24*
  - *The Rejoicing of Simeon 2:25–35*
  - *The Rejoicing of Anna 2:36–38*

The Amazing Early Years of Jesus 2:39–52

Jesus' Childhood in Nazareth 2:39–40

Jesus' Self-Awareness During a Notable Pilgrimage 2:41–50

- The Missing Jesus Found Teaching in the Temple 2:41–48
- His Explanation to His Parents of His Heavenly Father's Work 2:49–50

Summary of Jesus' Developmental Years with His Family 2:51–52

John's Momentous Baptism of the Son of God 3:1–38

The Preparatory Preaching of John the Baptist 3:1–20

- Summary of John's Ministry 3:1–6
- Samples of John's Preaching 3:7–18
- Record of John's Imprisonment 3:19–20

The Baptism of Jesus, the "Son" of God 3:21–22

- The Baptism in the Jordan 3:21
- Heavenly Attestation of Divine Sonship 3:22

The Genealogy of "the Son of God" 3:23–38

Satan's Failed Temptation of the Son of God 4:1–13

Driven by the Spirit into the Wilderness for Testing 4:1

Tempted by the Devil for Forty Days 4:2

Three Rounds of Satanic Temptation 4:3–12

Summary of Jesus' Success Against Satan's Efforts 4:13

MAIN BODY: 4:14–21:38

- Jesus' Ministry in Galilee: Jesus Revealed as Son of God & Man, 4:14–9:50
- Jesus' Ministry on The Way to Jerusalem: Disciples Prepared for Jesus' Rejection, 9:51–19:27
- The Ministry of Jesus In Jerusalem: Jesus Rejected & Jerusalem Doomed, 19:28–21:38

CONCLUSION: Dramatic Culmination to Jesus' Earthly Ministry, 22:1–24:53

CHART 14: Focus on Luke 4:14–9:50

INTRODUCTION: EXTENSIVE PROLOGUE TO JESUS' EARTHLY MINISTRY, 1:1–4:13

MAIN BODY: 4:14–21:38

JESUS' MINISTRY IN GALILEE: JESUS REVEALED AS SON OF GOD & MAN, 4:14–9:50

Beginning of the Ministry: Rejection, Relocation & Reception 4:14–44	The Calling of the Disciples & Creation of a New Community 5:1–6:49	The Revelation of Jesus to the Multitudes 7:1–8:56	The Disciples' Ministry Enlarged & Jesus' Mission Clarified 9:1–50
Summary of Early Ministry Success in Galilee 4:14–15 **Presentation & Rejection in Nazareth, His Hometown 4:16–30** Synagogue Reading of Isaiah's Prophecy & Its Fulfillment in Jesus 4:16–21 Explanation of Their Unbelief 4:22–27 Escape from Their Rage 4:28–30 **Ministry of Many Miracles 4:31–41** Deliverance of the Demoniac in the Capernaum Synagogue 4:31–37 Simon's Mother-in-Law Healed 4:38–39 Many Healed, Demons Rebuked 4:40–41 **Ministry in the Galilean Synagogues 4:42–44**	**Displaying Power & Growing Controve3rsy 5:1–6:16** The Miraculous Catch & the 4 Fisherman 5:1–11 Cleansing of a Leper & Healing a Paralytic 5:12–26 The Calling of Levi & Dining with Sinners 5:27–32 Controversy over Fasting & the Wineskins Parable 5:33–39 Lord of the Sabbath & the Synagogue Healing 6:1–11 The Appointing of the Twelve 6:12–16 **The Sermon on the Plain 6:17–49** Teaching to the Crowds 6:17–19 Blessings & Woes 6:20–26 The Call to Love Enemies 6:27–36 The Sin of Judging Others 6:37–42 Trees Known by Their Fruit 6:43–45 Foundations of Rock & Sand 6:46–49	**Questions of Jesus' Identity Answered 7:1–8:3** Healing of the Centurion's Servant 7:1–10 Raising of the Widow's Son at Nain 7:11–17 Answering John's Concerns & Affirming Him 7:18–30 A Generation's Rejection Described 7:31–35 Forgiveness of the Sinful Woman & Parable of the Two Debtors 7:36–50 Women in Jesus' Service as it Spreads 8:1–3 **Cryptic Revelations in the Parables 8:4–21** Parable of the Seed & Soils 8:4–15 Parable of the Lamp 8:16–18 Jesus' True Family 8:19–21 **Power Over the Natural & Supernatural 8:22–56** Calming of the Sea 8:22–25 Deliverance of the Gerasene Demoniac 8:26–39 Healing of the Twelves: The Girl & the Hemorrhage 8:40–56	**The Successful Mission of the Twelve 9:1–9** The Twelve Sent Out 9:1–6 Herod Perplexed by Jesus 9:7–9 **Jesus' Glory & the Path to Greatness 9:10–50** Feeding of the 5000 9:10–17 Peter's Confession of Christ 9:18–20 Prophecy of the Passion & the Painful Path of Discipleship 9:21–27 The Transfiguration 9:28–36 The Demoniac Boy Healed & the Disciples Exposed 9:37–43a Second Prophecy of the Passion 9:43b–45 Instructions on Kingdom Greatness & Ministry Cooperation 9:46–50

JESUS' MINISTRY ON THE WAY TO JERUSALEM: DISCIPLES PREPARED FOR JESUS' REJECTION, 9:51–19:27

THE MINISTRY OF JESUS IN JERUSALEM: JESUS REJECTED & JERUSALEM DOOMED, 19:28–21:38

CONCLUSION: DRAMATIC CULMINATION TO JESUS' EARTHLY MINISTRY, 22:1–24:53

CHART 15: Focus on Luke 9:51–13:21

INTRODUCTION: Extensive Prologue to Jesus' Earthly Ministry, 1:1–4:13

MAIN BODY: 4:14–21:38

Jesus' Ministry in Galilee: Jesus Revealed as Son of God & Man, 4:14–9:50

Jesus' Ministry on the Way to Jerusalem: Disciples Prepared for Jesus' Rejection, 9:51–19:27

Collection One from the Journey to Jerusalem: *Instructing the Disciples on Their Duties* 9:51–13:21

The Ministry Expanded in Samaria & by the Seventy 9:51–10:37	**Samplings of Ministry in Bethany & Judea 10:38–13:21**			
Rejection from a Samaritan Village 9:51–56	**Instructions on Discipleship 10:38–11:13**	**Conflicts & Controversies 11:14–54**	**Teachings to the Disciples in the Presence of the Crowds 12:1–53**	**Understanding the Times & the Lord's Will 12:54–13:21**
The Weeding Out of Half-Hearted Disciples 9:57–62 **The Mission of the Seventy 10:1–24** Instructions for Their Mission 10:1–12 Woes Pronounced on Unrepentant Cities 10:13–15 Authorization of Jesus' Messengers 10:16 Return & Report of the Seventy 10:17–20 Jesus' Thanksgiving & Blessing on the Seventy 10:21–24 **Parable of the Good Samaritan 10:25–37**	Mary, Martha & Choosing the Better Thing 10:38–42 Lessons on Prayer 11:1–13 *The Lord's Prayer 11:1–4* *Parable of the Midnight Request 11:5–8* *Instructions on Freely Asking & Trusting God 11:9–13*	The Beelzebul Accusation 11:14–28 *Exorcism of the Mute Demon 11:14* *Accusation of Satanic Power 11:15–16* *Jesus' Work as God's Finger 11:17–23* *Parable of the Returning Spirits 11:24–26* *Blessing on the Obedient 11:27–28* The Wicked Generation 11:29–36 *No Sign but Jonah 11:29–32* *Two Teachings on Light 11:33–36* Contra Pharisees & Scribes 11:37–54 *Woes on the Pharisees 11:37–44* *Woes on the Scribes 11:45–52* *Pharisees & Scribes Conspire 11:53–54*	Instructions on True Spirituality 12:1–12 *Warning against Hypocrisy 12:1–3* *Call to Fear & Trust God Alone 12:4–7* *Call to Confess Christ Boldly 12:8–12* Parable of the Rich Fool 12:13–21 Countermands to Anxiety 12:22–32 Call to Live Charitably 12:33–34 Readiness for the Son of Man's Coming 12:35–48 *Like Servants Waiting for Their Master 12:35–38* *Unlike the House Ill-Prepared for the Thief 12:39–40* *Like the Slave Found Doing His Master's Will 12:41–48* Jesus as the Cause of Inevitable Division 12:49–53	The Failure to Forecast the Times 12:54–56 The Urgency of Making Matters Right 12:57–59 The Urgency of Repentance 13:1–9 *Tragedy as a Wakeup Call to Repent 13:1–5* *Parable of the Fruitless Fig Tree & Coming Destruction 13:6–9* Controversy over Healing the Crippled Woman on the Sabbath 13:10–17 Two Kingdom Parables: Mustard Seed & Leaven 13:18–21

Collection Two from the Journey to Jerusalem: *Forming the Disciples in Their Character*, 13:22–17:10

Collection Three from the Journey to Jerusalem: *Preparing the Disciples for The Future*, 17:11–19:27

The Ministry of Jesus in Jerusalem: Jesus Rejected & Jerusalem Doomed, 19:28–21:38

CONCLUSION: Dramatic Culmination to Jesus' Earthly Ministry, 22:1–24:53

CHART 16: Focus on Luke 13:22–17:10

INTRODUCTION: EXTENSIVE PROLOGUE TO JESUS' EARTHLY MINISTRY, 1:1–4:13

MAIN BODY: 4:14–21:38

JESUS' MINISTRY IN GALILEE: JESUS REVEALED AS SON OF GOD & MAN, 4:14–9:50

JESUS' MINISTRY ON THE WAY TO JERUSALEM: DISCIPLES PREPARED FOR JESUS' REJECTION, 9:51–19:27

Collection One from the Journey to Jerusalem: *Instructing the Disciples on Their Duties*, 9:51–13:21

Collection Two from the Journey to Jerusalem:
Forming the Disciples in Their Character
13:22–17:10

The Narrow Way, Oppositions & Invitations 13:22–14:24		**Collection of Teachings to the Crowds, the Disciples & the Adversaries 14:25–17:10**			
Few to be Saved, Many to Perish 13:22–35	**Events at a Pharisee's Home 14:1–24**	**The Cost of Discipleship 14:25–35**	**God's Pursuit of Sinners 15:1–32**	**Lessons on Management & the Love of Money 16:1–31**	**Instructions on Discipleship 17:1–10**
The Narrow Way 13:22–30 *Question Over the Number of Those Saved 13:22–23* *Call to Enter the Narrow Gate 13:24* *Many Future Surprises of Rejection & Reward 13:24–30* Lament Over the Loss of Jerusalem 13:31–35 *Pharisees Seek to Frighten Him Away 13:31* *Jesus' Determination to Proceed to His Goal 13:32–33* *Jesus' Lament 13:34–35*	Healing of Dropsy on the Sabbath 14:1–6 Lessons on Humility at the Banquet 14:7–14 *Seek the Least Spot 14:7–11* *Invite the Least Likely 14:12–14* Parable of the Great Banquet 14:15–24 *Anticipation of the Kingdom Banquet 14:15* *Warning Not to Spurn the Banquet's Invitation 14:16–24*	The Large Crowd to be Thinned 14:25 The Call to Love Christ More than Family 14:26 The Call to Carry the Cross 14:27 The Call to Count the Cost 14:28–33 *Parable of the Builder 14:28–30* *Parable of the King at War 14:31–32* *The Need to Forsake All for Christ 14:33* False Disciples Likened to Savorless Salt 14:34–35	Jesus Criticized for Welcoming Sinners 15:1–2 Jesus' Instruction on God's Pursuit of Sinners 15:3–32 *Parable of the Lost Sheep 15:1–7* *Parable of the Lost Coin 15:8–10* *Parable of the Lost Son 15:11–32* Loss & Return of the Prodigal Son 15:11–24 Lesson for the Older Son 15:25–32	Parable of the Shrewd Manager 16:1–8 Instruction on Wise Stewardship 16:9–13 *The Righteous Use of Money 16:9* *Faithfulness in Managing Lesser Things 16:10–12* *Serving God over Money 16:13* Indictment of the Greedy Pharisees 16:14–18 The Parable of the Rich Man & Lazarus 16:19–31	The Disciples Addressed 17:1a Warning Against False Teaching 17:1b–3a Lessons on Confron-tation & Forgiveness 17:3b–4 The Power of Even Little Faith 17:5–6 Parable of the Unworthy Servant 17:7–10

Collection Three from the Journey to Jerusalem: *Preparing the Disciples for The Future*, 17:11–19:27

THE MINISTRY OF JESUS IN JERUSALEM: JESUS REJECTED & JERUSALEM DOOMED, 19:28–21:38

CONCLUSION: DRAMATIC CULMINATION TO JESUS' EARTHLY MINISTRY, 22:1–24:53

CHART 17: Focus on Luke 17:11–19:27

INTRODUCTION: EXTENSIVE PROLOGUE TO JESUS' EARTHLY MINISTRY, 1:1–4:13

MAIN BODY: 4:14–21:38

JESUS' MINISTRY IN GALILEE: JESUS REVEALED AS SON OF GOD & MAN, 4:14–9:50

JESUS' MINISTRY ON THE WAY TO JERUSALEM: DISCIPLES PREPARED FOR JESUS' REJECTION 9:51–19:27

Collection One from the Journey to Jerusalem: *Instructing the Disciples on Their Duties*, 9:51–13:21

Collection Two from the Journey to Jerusalem: *Forming the Disciples in Their Character*, 13:22–17:10

Collection Three from the Journey to Jerusalem: *Preparing the Disciples for The Future* 17:11–19:27

The Mercy of the King & the Coming Kingdom 17:11–18:8	Grace to the Humble & Reward for Service 18:9–18:30	The King's Coming Rejection, Saving Power & the Delayed Kingdom 18:31–19:27
The Ten Cleansed Lepers & the Grateful Samaritan 17:11–19	Parable of the Pharisee & the Tax Collector 18:9–14	Third Foretelling of Jesus' Passion 18:31–34
Answers about the Coming Kingdom 17:20–37	Jesus' Blessing of the Children 18:15–17	The Healed Beggar at Jericho who Discerns Jesus as Son of David 19:35–43
Question from the Pharisees & Jesus' Basic Reply 17:20–21	Interaction with the Rich Young Ruler 18:18–30	The Conversion of Zacchaeus, the Tax Collector 19:1–10
The Kingdom's Quick Coming Along with Judgment 17:22–37	*Jesus & the Ruler Interact 18:18–25*	Parable on Stewardship: The Ten Minas 19:11–27
Parable of the Persistent Widow & the Unjust Judge 18:1–8	*Follow-up Discussion with the Disciples 18:26–30*	

THE MINISTRY OF JESUS IN JERUSALEM: JESUS REJECTED & JERUSALEM DOOMED, 19:28–21:38

CONCLUSION: DRAMATIC CULMINATION TO JESUS' EARTHLY MINISTRY, 22:1–24:53

CHART 18: Focus on Luke 19:28–21:38

Introduction: Extensive Prologue to Jesus' Earthly Ministry, 1:1–4:13

MAIN BODY: 4:14–21:38

Jesus' Ministry in Galilee: Jesus Revealed as Son of God & Man, 4:14–9:50

Jesus' Ministry on the Way to Jerusalem: Disciples Prepared for Jesus' Rejection, 9:51–19:27

The Ministry of Jesus in Jerusalem: Jesus Rejected & Jerusalem Doomed 19:28–21:38				
Controversy Stirred in Jerusalem 19:28–21:4		**The Olivet Discourse & the Temple's Destruction 21:5–38**		
The Triumphal Entry 19:28–40 **Jesus' Lament Over Jerusalem 19:41–44** **The Cleansing of the Temple 19:45–46** **Teaching the Pilgrim Crowds 19:47–48**	**Controversies with the Religious Leadership 20:1–21:4** Jesus' Authority Questioned by the Religious Leadership 20:1–8 Parable of the Wicked Vinedressers 20:9–19 Answering the Scribes' & Chief Priests' Trick Question About Caesar's Tax 20:20–26 Answering the Sadducees' Trick Question About Resurrection 20:27–40 Stumping the Scribes on the Question about Messiah Being David's Son 20:41–44 Warning to the People about the Scribes 20:45–47 Lesson from the Widow's Two Mites 21:1–4	**The Future Fall of the Temple & the End of Time 21:5–24** The Setting 21:5 Prophecy of the Temple's Destruction 21:6 Signs Before the Temple's Destruction 21:7–9 Signs Before the End of Time: War & Persecution 21:10–19 The Coming Destruction that Foreshadows the End 21:20–24	**The Final Coming of the Son of Man 21:25–36** Prophecy of the Son of Man Coming in a Cloud 21:25–28 Parable of the Fig Tree 21:29–33 Call to Spiritual Vigilance 21:34–36	**Transition 21:37–38** Teaching in the Temple & His Strategic Nightly Withdrawal 21:37 Growing Interest by the Pilgrim Crowds 21:38

Conclusion: Dramatic Culmination to Jesus' Earthly Ministry, 22:1–24:53

CHART 19: Focus on Luke 22:1–24:53

INTRODUCTION: EXTENSIVE PROLOGUE TO JESUS' EARTHLY MINISTRY, 1:1–4:13

MAIN BODY: 4:14–21:38

- JESUS' MINISTRY IN GALILEE: JESUS REVEALED AS SON OF GOD & MAN, 4:14–9:50
- JESUS' MINISTRY ON THE WAY TO JERUSALEM: DISCIPLES PREPARED FOR JESUS' REJECTION, 9:51–19:27
- THE MINISTRY OF JESUS IN JERUSALEM: JESUS REJECTED & JERUSALEM DOOMED, 19:28–21:38

CONCLUSION: DRAMATIC CULMINATION TO JESUS' EARTHLY MINISTRY 22:1–24:53

The Passion of the Lord 22:1–23:56			The Resurrection, Commission & Ascension 24:1–53	
The Enemies' Plot & Jesus' Preparations 22:1–46	**The Arrest & Trials of Jesus 22:47–23:25**	**The Crucifixion & Burial of Jesus 23:26–56**	**The Resurrection Announced & Confirmed 24:1–43**	**The Great Commission & the Lord's Ascension 24:44–53**
Judas Joins the Passover Plot 22:1–6 Jesus' Preparations for Passover & the Last Supper 22:7–13 The Last Passover Observed 22:14–18 The Lord's Supper Instituted 22:19–20 Prophecy of Jesus' Betrayal 22:21–23 Dispute Over the Greatest in the Kingdom 22:24–30 Peter's Denials Foretold 22:31–34 God's Provision & Sure Rejection 21:35–38 Agonizing Prayer on the Mount of Olives 21:39–46	Jesus' Arrest 22:47–53 *Judas' Arrival with the Troops 22:47–48* *Jesus' Calming of the Scuffle & Healing of the Slave's Ear 22:49–53* Jesus Brought before the High Priest 22:54 Peter's "Trial" & His Three Denials 22:55–62 Jesus Mocked & Beaten by Guards 22:63–65 Conviction of Jesus by the Sanhedrin 22:66–71 Trial before Pilate 23:1–5 Trial before Herod 23:6–12 Pilate's Sentencing of Jesus 23:13–25 *Jesus' Innocence 23:13–16 [17]* *The Crowd's Choice of Barabbas 23:18–23* *Pilate's Release of Barabbas & Condemnation of Jesus 22:24–25*	The Execution of Jesus 23:26–44 *The Procession to the Site 23:26–31* Simon of Cyrene Made to Bear the Cross 23:26 Jesus' Words to the Weeping Women 23:27–31 *The Crucifixion of the King with Two Criminals 23:32–43* The Death of Jesus 23:44–49 Three Hours of Darkness 23:44 The Temple Veil Torn 23:45 Jesus' Prayer of Committal 23:46 The Centurion's Testimony of Innocence 23:47 The Mourning Witnesses of His Death 23:48–49 The Honorable Burial by Joseph & the Women 23:50–56	Discovery of the Resurrection 24:1–12 *Angelic Explanation of the Empty Tomb 24:1–7* *Report of the Women to the Apostles 24:8–11* *Peter's Testimony of the Empty Tomb 24:12* The Road to Emmaus & Jesus' Disclosure 24:13–35 *Two Men Met on the Road 24:13–16* *Jesus' Conversation & Exposition 24:17–27* *Jesus' Self-Revelation & Disappearance at the Meal 24:28–32* *The Two Report to the Apostles 24:33–35* Jesus' Appearance to the Disciples at a Meal 24:36–43	The Great Commission 24:44–48 The Promise of the Holy Spirit's Coming 24:49 Jesus' Ascension into Heaven 24:50–53

THE GOSPEL OF JOHN

John's Gospel is the most unique of the four, written by the Apostle John late in the first century (c. AD 90). He wrote for Jewish readers and God-fearing Gentiles in the region of Ephesus in Asia Minor. John reportedly moved to Ephesus shortly before the fall of Jerusalem in AD 70, and there he exercised apostolic authority for the next several decades. Near the end of that era he began to write the five books credited to him, including the final Gospel. Judaism was in a state of crisis with the destruction of the Temple, so this was an opportune time for John to reflect on and press home the claims of Jesus' Messianic identity in a fresh way. His Gospel includes many OT citations and allusions which reinforce his arguments.

John was one of the Twelve disciples in Jesus' inner circle, and thus was able to reveal more of Jesus' inner thoughts than the others. John humbly refers to himself throughout the book as, "the disciple whom Jesus loved" (John 13:23). The early church almost universally accepted this writing as an authentic piece from his hand, the biggest exception being early heretical groups which rejected the deity of Christ.

John stresses the deity of Jesus more frequently and clearly than any of the other Gospels. Indeed, his greatest burden was to demonstrate to the reader the reality that Jesus is God, and eternal life is available through faith in Him. This purpose is expressed clearly near the end of the book: "These have been written so that you may believe that Jesus is the Christ, the Son of God; and that believing you may have life in His name" (20:31).

When John wrote his Gospel, he knew that the other three told the story of Jesus in a somewhat synoptic fashion. Because John wished to cover ground the others did not include, over 90% of his work contains acts and sayings of Jesus not found elsewhere. The portions that are most similar are the passion and resurrection stories.

John also includes seven unique discourses of Jesus that highlight the importance of faith, discipleship, walking in God's light and truth, and being distinct from the world. In John's work, we hear Jesus most clearly explain the true nature of faith and how to attain everlasting life.

The book neatly divides into two halves. After a rich introduction focusing on Jesus' incarnation (1:1–18), the first half focuses on Jesus' public disclosure through His ministry (1:19–12:50). A series of numerous stories show how Jesus miraculously attested His identity in Galilee and Samaria (1:19–4:54). Opposition to Jesus mounts as seen in His repeated run-ins with Jewish authorities in Jerusalem at various festivals (5:1–12:50). While John records many miracles of Jesus, there are six notable ones in this first half of the book which he labels as "signs." The seventh and greatest sign, Jesus' resurrection, is reserved for the latter part of the book.

The second half focuses on Jesus' private disclosures to His disciples (13:1–20:31). Jesus earnestly prepared His disciples for the passion which was quickly coming (13:1–17:26). Though there is much they did not grasp, He promised to send the Spirit later to lead them more fully into an understanding of the truth. In the passion story, the identity of Jesus is fully displayed in His glorious resurrection after suffering an unjust death (18:1–20:31). In the book's conclusion (21:1–25), Jesus commissioned the disciples for the future years of service and sacrifice they would endure for His name.

CHART 20 **John** 	***Purpose***: John presents selected authenticating signs and significant discourses from Jesus' life & ministry that showed him to be the very Son of God and the only source of everlasting life for all who trust in Him.	***Date:*** *c.* AD 90 ***Recipients:*** Unbelieving Jews & God-fearers ***Author:*** John, ministering in Ephesus

PROLOGUE: THE INCARNATION OF THE ETERNAL SON OF GOD 1:1–18	**BODY OF THE GOSPEL: THE DISCLOSURE OF THE SON OF GOD 1:19–20:31**				**EPILOGUE: THE COMMISSION OF THE RESURRECTED SAVIOR 21:1–25**
	THE BOOK OF SIGNS: THE SON'S DISCLOSURE THRU THE DEEDS OF HIS MINISTRY 1:19–12:50		**THE BOOK OF GLORY: THE SON'S DISCLOSURE THRU HIS DISCOURSES & PASSION 13:1–20:31**		
The Eternal Word's Action in Creation 1:1–5 **John the Baptist's Witness to Jesus as the Light 1:6–8** **Jesus' Incarnation as Light & Life 1:9–14** **John the Baptist's Witness to Jesus' Supremacy 1:15** **Jesus as God's Revelation of Grace & Truth 1:16–18**	**Miraculous Presentations of Jesus as the Son of God 1:19–4:54** The Amazing First Week 1:19–2:11 *John the Baptist's Prophetic Testimony 1:19–34* *The Magnetic Call of the Disciples 1:35–51* *Miracle at Cana:* ***The First Sign*** *2:1–12* A Circuit of Miraculous Ministry 2:13–4:54 *Ministry in Judea:* ***The Final Sign Foretold*** *2:13–3:36* *Ministry in Samaria: The Living Water 4:1–42* *Ministry in Galilee:* ***The Second Sign*** *4:43–54*	**Mounting Opposition to Jesus by the Jews at Festivals 5:1–12:50** Sabbath Healing of the Lame Man in Jerusalem at a Feast: **The Third Sign** 5:1–47 The Bread of Heaven Feeds the 5,000 During Passover: **The Fourth Sign** 6:1–71 Controversies in Jerusalem 7:1–12:50 *At Tabernacles: The Light of the World Rejected 7:1–8:59* *At Dedication: The Healing of the Blind Man Opposed,* ***The Fifth Sign*** *9:1–10:42* *Before Passover: The Plot to Kill Jesus, Who Raises Lazarus,* ***The Sixth Sign*** *11:1–12:50*	**The Disciples Prepared thru Jesus' Private Disclosures 13:1–17:26** Preparation of the Passover & the Final Betrayal 13:1–30 *The Loving Example of the Betrayed Servant 13:1–20* *The Foretelling of the Betrayal to the Disciples 13:21–30* Preparation of the Disciples in the Farewell Discourse in the Final Passover 13:31–16:33 *In the Upper Room 13:31–14:31* *In Route to Gethsemane 15:1–16:33* Preparation of the Disciples in the Intercession of Jesus' Final Prayer 17:1–26	**Jesus' Glory Disclosed thru His Passion & Resurrection 18:1–20:31** The "Hour" of the King Commenced with the Shame of Crucifixion 18:1–19:42 *Arrest in Gethsemane 18:1–12* *Jewish & Roman Trials 18:13–19:16* *Crucifixion & Burial 19:17–42* The "Hour" of the King Consummated in the Glory of Resurrection 20:1–31 *The Empty Tomb 20:1–10* *Appearances to Mary & the Disciples:* ***The Final Sign*** *20:11–29* *The Purpose of the Book 20:30–31*	**Appearance to the Disciples in Galilee 21:1–14** The 7 Disciples by the Sea 21:1–3 The Great Catch 21:4–8 Meal with the Resurrected Savior 21:9–14 **The Restoration of Peter & His Future Foretold 21:15–19** **John's Long Ministry Foretold 21:20–23** **John's Concluding Witness 21:24–25**

CHART 21: Focus on John 1:19–4:54

PROLOGUE: The Incarnation of the Eternal Son of God, 1:1–18

BODY OF THE GOSPEL: The Disclosure of the Son of God, 1:19–20:31

THE BOOK OF SIGNS: The Son's Disclosure thru the Deeds of His Ministry, 1:19–12:50

Miraculous Presentations of Jesus as the Son of God 1:19–4:54

The Amazing First Week 1:19–2:11			A Circuit of Miraculous Ministry 2:12–4:54				
			Ministry in Judea: THE FINAL SIGN FORETOLD 2:13–3:36				
John the Baptist's Prophetic Testimony 1:19–34	**The Magnetic Call of the Disciples 1:35–51**	**Miracle at Cana: THE FIRST SIGN 2:1–12**	**The Cleansing of the Temple & the First Passover 2:13–25**	**Nicodemus Instructed on the New Birth 3:1–21**	**The Final Word of the Forerunner 3:22–36**	**Ministry in Samaria: The Living Water 4:1–42**	**Ministry in Galilee: THE SECOND SIGN 4:43–54**
John Disavows Messianic Claims & Diverts Attention 1:19–28 John Identifies Jesus as Messiah 1:29–34	John Transfers Two Disciples to Jesus 1:35–39 The Addition of Simon Peter & His New Name 1:40–42 The Additions of Phillip & Nathaniel 1:43–51 *The Move Toward Galilee 1:43–44* *Nathaniel's Reluctance & Jesus' Overwhelming Insights 1:45–51*	The Setting of the Wedding 2:1–2 The Short Run of Wine 2:3–5 Obedience to Jesus' Instruction 2:6–9 The Waiter's Amazement at Water Turned to Wine 2:10–11 The Rest of the Week with Jesus' Family 2:12	Jesus' Zeal to Cleanse Temple Corruption 2:13–17 Jesus as the Meeting Point Between God & Men 2:18–22 *The Authority of Jesus as the Embodied Temple 2:18–21* *The Disciples' Later Understanding of the Prophecy 2:22* Fame at Passover & the People's Fickleness 2:23–25	A Secret Arrival & Searching Statement 3:1–2 Explanation of the New Birth 3:3–9 Jesus' Discourse on Everlasting Life 3:10–21 *Jesus, the Son Come Down, Soon to be Lifted Up 3:10–15* *Jesus, the Life-changing Gift to All Who Believe 3:16–21*	The Intersection of Jesus' & John's Ministries in Judea 3:22–24 The Concern of John's Disciples about Jesus 3:25–26 John's Final Discourse in the Book: The Need for Jesus to Increase at All Costs 3:27–36	The Setting: A Sojourn in Samaria with a Stop at Sychar 4:1–6 The Unconventional Interchange with the Woman at the Well 4:7–26 *The Request for a Drink & the Discourse on Living Water 4:7–14* *The Prophetic Validation of Jesus as the Messiah 4:15–26* The Aftermath of the Interchange 4:27–42 *The Curiosity of the Disciples 4:27* *The Evangelism of the Woman to the People of the City 4:28–30* *The Satisfaction of the Savior & His Call to Evangelistic Mission 4:31–38* *Faith in Messiah Kindled Amongst the Samaritans 4:39–42*	Reception in Galilee after Rejection in Jerusalem 4:43–45 Healing of the Nobleman's Son 4:46–54 *The Return to Cana & the Nobleman's Plea for His Dying Son 4:46–47* *Jesus' Concern about the Quest for Signs 4:48* *Jesus' Remote Healing of the Boy as the Second Sign 4:49–54*

Mounting Opposition to Jesus by the Jews at Festivals, 5:1–12:50

THE BOOK OF GLORY: The Son's Disclosure thru His Discourses & Passion, 13:1–20:31

EPILOGUE: The Commission of the Resurrected Savior, 21:1–25

CHART 22: Focus on John 5:1–8:59

PROLOGUE: THE INCARNATION OF THE ETERNAL SON OF GOD, 1:1–18

BODY OF THE GOSPEL: THE DISCLOSURE OF THE SON OF GOD, 1:19–20:31

THE BOOK OF SIGNS: THE SON'S DISCLOSURE THRU THE DEEDS OF HIS MINISTRY, 1:19–12:50

Miraculous Presentations of Jesus as the Son of God, 1:19–4:54

Mounting Opposition to Jesus by the Jews at Festivals 5:1–12:50

Controversies in Jerusalem, 7:1–12:50

At Tabernacles: The Light of the World Rejected 7:1–8:59

Sabbath Healing of the Lame Man in Jerusalem at a Feast: THE THIRD SIGN 5:1–47	**The Bread of Heaven Feeds the 5,000 During Passover: THE FOURTH SIGN 6:1–71**	**First Cycle of Controversies 7:1–[8:11]**	**Second Cycle of Controversies 8:12–59**
Healing by the Pool of Bethesda 5:1–9a	Public Miracles by the Sea 6:1–15	The Setting: Jesus' Unbelieving Brothers & His Secret Arrival 7:1–13	The Light of the World Rejected 8:12–20
The Setting 5:1–5	*The Setting by the Sea of Galilee: A Period of Miraculous Ministry 6:1–4*	Accusations against Jesus in the Middle of Tabernacles 7:14–36	Jesus' Announcement of His Departure to the Father 8:21–30
Healing by Jesus' Word 5:6–9a	*The Feeding of the 5,000 6:5–13*	*Jesus, the Untrained Teacher 7:14–18*	*Warning about Remaining in Unbelief 8:21–24*
Controversy Over Healing on the Sabbath 5:9b–29	*The Withdrawal of Jesus to Prevent Insurrection 6:14–15*	*Jesus, the Deluded Demoniac 7:19–24*	*Jesus' Association with the Father 8:25–30*
The Jews' Inquest into the Healing 5:9b–16	Private Miracle on the Sea: Jesus Walks on Water 6:16–21	*Jesus, the Impossible Messiah 7:25–29*	Jesus' Enemies Enslaved to Sin 8:31–59
Jesus' Defense of His Equality with God & His Unique Mission 5:17–23	Discourse on the Bread of Heaven 6:22–59	*The Plan to Arrest Jesus 7:30–36*	*True Freedom in Following Christ 8:31–32*
Jesus' Self-Identification as Source of Eternal Life & the Final Judge 5:24–30	*The Crowd's Search for Jesus 6:22–25*	The Final Festival Day & the Rejection of Living Water 7:37–52	*Jewish Rejection of Jesus' Freedom 8:33–38*
The Four-Fold Witness to Jesus 5:31–47	*The Crowd's Search for a Sign 6:26–34*	*The Offer of Living Water 7:37–39*	*Unbelieving Sons of Abraham Called Children of the Devil 8:39–47*
The Testimony of John the Baptist 5:31–35	*The Bread of Life Rejected 6:35–59*	*Varying Opinions about Jesus & a Failed Arrest 7:40–52*	*Accusation of Demon Possession & Jesus' Claim of Deity 8:48–58*
The Testimony of Jesus' Works 5:36	The Desertion of Many Disciples 6:60–66	[The Adulteress Forgiven 7:53–8:11]	*The Attempt to Stone Jesus 8:59*
The Testimony of the Father 5:37–38	The Confession of Peter & the Foretelling of Judas' Betrayal 6:67–71		
The Testimony of Scripture 5:39–47			

At Dedication: The Healing of the Blind Man Opposed, The Fifth Sign, 9:1–10:42

Before Passover: The Plot to Kill Jesus who Raises Lazarus, The Sixth Sign, 11:1–12:50

THE BOOK OF GLORY: THE SON'S DISCLOSURE THRU HIS DISCOURSES & PASSION, 13:1–20:31

EPILOGUE: THE COMMISSION OF THE RESURRECTED SAVIOR, 21:1–25

CHART 23: Focus on John 9:1–12:50

PROLOGUE: The Incarnation of the Eternal Son of God, 1:1–18

BODY OF THE GOSPEL: The Disclosure of the Son of God, 1:19–20:31

THE BOOK OF SIGNS: The Son's Disclosure thru the Deeds of His Ministry, 1:19–12:50

Miraculous Presentations of Jesus as the Son of God, 1:19–4:54

Mounting Opposition to Jesus by the Jews at Festivals
5:1–12:50

Sabbath Healing of the Lame Man in Jerusalem at a Feast: The Third Sign, 5:1–47

The Bread of Heaven Feeds the 5,000 During Passover: The Fourth Sign, 6:1–71

Controversies in Jerusalem
7:1–12:50

At Tabernacles: The Light of the World is Rejected, 7:1–8:59

At Dedication: The Healing of the Blind Man Opposed, THE FIFTH SIGN 9:1–10:42

The Healing of the Blind Man & the Problem of Spiritual Blindness
9:1–41

The Light of the World Illumines the Man Born Blind
9:1–7

Controversies over the Healing
9:8–34

The Confusion of His Neighbors
9:8–12

Double Interrogation by Unbelieving Pharisees
9:13–34

Jesus' Disclosure to the Healed Man
9:35–38

Jesus' Indictment of the Blind Pharisees
9:39–41

The Good Shepherd & the Spiritual Perception of His Sheep
10:1–42

The Parable Set Forth & Explained
10:1–18

Mixed Response of Accusers & Believers
10:19–21

Controversy at the Feast
10:22–42

The Demand for Messianic Identification
10:22–24

The Ability of Sheep to Identify the Shepherd
10:25–29

Jesus' Identification with the Father
10:30

Failed Attempts to Counter & Neutralize Jesus
10:31–42

Before Passover: The Plot to Kill Jesus, Who Raises Lazarus, THE SIXTH SIGN 11:1–12:50

The Miracle before Passover & the Passover Plot
11:1–57

The Raising of Lazarus from the Dead
11:1–46

The Call for Jesus to Heal Lazarus & Jesus' Intentional Delay
11:1–10

The Death of Lazarus Explained
11:11–16

The Arrival of Jesus Amongst Mourners & His Announcement of Resurrection
11:17–37

The Raising of Lazarus from the Tomb
11:38–44

Reactions & Reports of the Miracle
11:45–46

The Official Plot to Kill Jesus
11:47–57

The Sanhedrin's Plot with an Unwitting Prophecy of Jesus' Sacrifice
11:47–53

The Withdrawal of Jesus & Jerusalem's Mixed Anticipation Regarding His Return
11:54–57

The Preparation of the Lamb
12:1–50

Jesus' Anointing for Death Amidst a Plot
12:1–11

Reactions to Jesus' Entry to Jerusalem:
12:12–22

The Acclamation of the Crowd
12:12–15

The Ignorance of the Disciples
12:16

The Disdain of the Pharisees
12:17–19

The Embrace of the Greek God-Fearers
12:20–22

Jesus' Perspective on His Hour Come
12:23–50

The Invitation to Death & Eternal Life
12:23–26

Jesus' Agony & Heaven's Affirmation of His Suffering & Future Glory
12:27–36

Prophetic Explanation of Jesus' Rejection
12:37–43

Jesus' Final Call to the Crowds
12:44–50

THE BOOK OF GLORY: The Son's Disclosure thru His Discourses & Passion, 13:1–20:31

EPILOGUE: The Commission of the Resurrected Savior, 21:1–25

CHART 24: Focus on John 13:1–17:26

PROLOGUE: THE INCARNATION OF THE ETERNAL SON OF GOD, 1:1–18

THE BOOK OF SIGNS: THE SON'S DISCLOSURE THRU THE DEEDS OF HIS MINISTRY, 1:19–12:50

BODY OF THE GOSPEL: THE DISCLOSURE OF THE SON OF GOD, 1:19–20:31

THE BOOK OF GLORY: THE SON'S DISCLOSURE THRU HIS DISCOURSES & PASSION, 13:1–17:26

The Disciples Prepared thru Jesus' Private Disclosures 13:1–17:26

Preparation of the Passover & the Final Betrayal 13:1–30	**Preparation of the Disciples in the Farewell Discourse in the Final Passover 13:31–16:33**				**Preparation of the Disciples in the Intercession of Jesus' Final Prayer 17:1–26**
	In the Upper Room 13:31–14:31		**In Route to Gethsemane 15:1–16:33**		
The Loving Example of the Betrayed Servant 13:1–20 *Jesus' Awareness of the Time 13:1–4* *Jesus' Washing of the Disciples' Feet 13:5–11* *Foot Washing as a Living Parable of Servanthood 13:12–20* The Foretelling of the Betrayal to the Disciples 13:21–30 *The Agonizing Disclosure & the Disciples' Inquiry 13:21–25* *The Satanic Overthrow of Judas & His Departure 13:26–30*	**Jesus' Announce-ment of the Hour 13:31–35** The Glory at Hand 13:31–32 Jesus' Soon Departure & the Need to Love One Another 13:33–35	**The Disciples' Questions 13:36–14:24** Peter's Quest to Follow Jesus, Jesus' Prophecy of His Failure & Jesus' Confidence in Their End 13:36–14:4 Thomas' Uncertainty on Where to Go & Jesus' Identification of Himself as the Way 14:5–7 Philip's Request to See the Father & Jesus' Teaching on Abiding in Himself & Relying on the Coming Spirit 14:8–21 Judas' Confusion about Jesus' Private Disclosure & Jesus' Teaching on Those Who Abide 14:22–24 **The Promise of the Coming Spirit & Christ's Peace 14:25–31**	**The Parable of the Vine & the Branches: Abiding in Christ 15:1–11** The Image Set Forth 15:1–6 The Imagery Applied to Abiding in Jesus' Words 15:7–11 **The Disciples' Future Experience with Love & Hate 15:12–25** The Command to Love One Another & the Example of Jesus' Sacrificial Love 15:12–17 The World's Hatred of Jesus to be Extended to His Disciples 15:18–25	**The Promise of the Spirit's Work 15:26–16:15** The Spirit's Future Witness & Aid to Their Witness amidst Persecution 15:26–16:4a The Spirit's Future Work of Conviction & Judgment 16:4b–11 The Spirit's Leadership of the Disciples into Further Truth 16:12–15 **Prophecy of Soon-Coming Grief & Joy for His Death & Resurrection 16:16–33** The Disciples' Confusion about "Soon" 16:16–19 The Illustration of Childbirth 16:20–22 The Privilege of Prayer thru Jesus 16:23–28 The Coming Desertion & the Promise of Peace & Victory 16:29–33	Prayer to Finish His Glorious Mission 17:1–5 *For Glorification in the Completion of His Mission 17:1–3* *For the Restoration of Divine Glory after His Mission 17:4–5* Prayer for His Disciples Remaining Behind 17:6–19 *Thanks for the Father's Entrustment of the Disciples 17:6–8* *Prayer for God's Preservation 17:9–15* *Prayer for Their Holiness in the Midst of Their Mission 17:16–19* Prayer for the Unity of the Future Church 17:20–23 Prayer for the Disciples' Future in Glory 17:24 Concluding Prayer of Love 17:25–26

Jesus' Glory Disclosed thru His Passion & Resurrection, 18:1–20:31

EPILOGUE: THE COMMISSION OF THE RESURRECTED SAVIOR, 21:1–25

CHART 25: Focus on John 18:1–20:31

PROLOGUE: THE INCARNATION OF THE ETERNAL SON OF GOD, 1:1–18

BODY OF THE GOSPEL: THE DISCLOSURE OF THE SON OF GOD, 1:19–20:31

THE BOOK OF SIGNS: THE SON'S DISCLOSURE THRU THE DEEDS OF HIS MINISTRY, 1:19–12:50

THE BOOK OF GLORY: THE SON'S DISCLOSURE THRU HIS DISCOURSES & PASSION, 13:1–17:26

The Disciples Prepared thru Jesus' Private Disclosures, 13:1–17:26

Jesus' Glory Disclosed thru His Passion & Resurrection 18:1–20:31

The "Hour" of the King Commenced with the Shame of Crucifixion 18:1–19:42				The Hour of the King Consummated in the Glory of Resurrection 20:1–31	The Purpose of the Book 20:30–31
Arrest in Gethsemane 18:1–12	**Jewish & Roman Trials 18:13–19:16**		**Crucifixion & Burial 19:17–42**	**The Empty Tomb 20:1–10**	
	The Jewish Trials & the Testing of Peter 18:13–27	**The Roman Trial 18:28–19:16**			
Jesus Retreats to a Garden with the Disciples 18:1 The Arrival of Judas with Arresting Forces 18:2–3 Jesus' Word Overpowers the Band 18:4–9 Peter's Violent Attempt to Protect Jesus 18:10–11 Jesus Arrested & Bound 18:12	The Setting at Annas' House 13:13–14 Peter's Initial Denial 18:15–18 Jesus Interrogated by Annas 18:19–23 Jesus Remanded to Caiaphas 18:24 Peter's Second & Third Denials 18:25–27	Jesus Remanded by Caiaphas to Pilate 18:28 Pilate's Hesitant Initial Interrogation of the King 18:29–38 The Crowd's Selection of Barabbas as a Substitute 18:39–40	The King's Crucifixion 19:17–27 *The Setting & Circumstances 19:17–18* *The Royal Inscription on the Cross 19:19–22* *The Prophecy of Confiscation Fulfilled 19:23–25a* *Jesus' Arrangements for His Mother 19:25b–27* The Death of Jesus 19:28–37 *The Final Drink & the Final Utterance 19:28–30* *Confirmation of Death & the Piercing of the Lamb 19:31–37* The King's Honorable Burial Pursued by Joseph of Arimathea & Nicodemus 19:38–42	Mary Magdalene's Discovery of the Empty, Opened Tomb 20:1–2 Peter & John's Investigation of the Empty Tomb 20:3–10 **Appearances to Mary & the Disciples: THE FINAL SIGN 20:11–29** The Appearance to Mary Magdalene 20:11–18 *The Angelic Visitation 20:11–13* *The Appearance of Jesus 20:14–18* The Appearances in the Upper Room 20:19–31 *The Appearance to the Disciples & the Breathing Out of the Spirit 20:19–23* *The Appearance to Thomas & a Blessing on Those Who Believe Without Sight 20:24–29*	The Book's Exclusion of Many of Jesus' Signs 20:30 The Book's Signs Selected to Promote Belief in Jesus as God's Son & Savior 20:31

EPILOGUE: THE COMMISSION OF THE RESURRECTED SAVIOR, 21:1–25

THE BOOK OF ACTS

The book of Acts, written by Luke during Paul's Roman imprisonment (AD 61–63), details the progress of the gospel and the growth of the church among Jews and Gentiles. It is a continuation of Luke's Gospel which ends with Jesus' commissioning the disciples to spread the news of His saving work.

Luke was a companion of the Apostle Paul and was an eyewitness to many of the stories in the second half of Acts. The various "we" passages beginning at Acts 16:10 act as important textual markers placing the author himself in the stories. Luke accompanied Paul to Rome to await his trial before Caesar, and at some point, encountered Theophilus. While this man's identity has been much debated, Luke's reference to him as "most excellent" (Luke 1:3; cf. Acts 23:26; 24:3; 26:25) suggests he was a Gentile of high social order. He was likely a convert of Paul's ministry and perhaps a supporter of the same. Luke wrote his Gospel and Acts to this man who needed clarification that the gospel was truly God-ordained for Gentiles like himself. The collection of historical narratives in Acts would help Theophilus better understand the growth of the church amongst gospel-believing Jews and Gentiles.

Luke does not attempt to write a complete history of the church's first 30 years, choosing rather to focus on the ministries of Peter and Paul. The larger purpose of the book is to validate Paul's ministry to the Gentiles, a mission which met great resistance in Jewish circles. The book begins by focusing on Peter's ministry, but the remaining two thirds is about Paul's. Peter and most of the other apostles were active in ministry during Paul's missionary journeys, but Luke has special interest in Paul's work, showing it as an extension of Jesus' work.

This understanding of Luke's purpose elucidates the book's structure. It does not flow so much around points of geography (Jerusalem, Judea, Samaria, etc.), but around the ministries of Peter and Paul. The book opens with a Prologue (1:1–11) that reminds Theophilus of the earlier Gospel volume. In the first half of the book (1:12–12:24), Luke focuses on Peter's leadership of the early church from Pentecost to the beginnings of the mission to the Gentiles. Toward the end of the accounts of Peter's ministry, Saul (later Paul) is introduced, first as a persecutor and then as a convert to Christ. The book then shifts focus onto Paul's ministry until the end (12:25–28:31). Peter's last appearance in the narrative is at the Jerusalem Council where he validates Paul's ministry to the Gentiles (15:1–16:4).

The two halves of the book both contain three sub-sections, each concluding with a summary statement about the progress of the Gospel. The book does not have a fully developed conclusion, but the final sub-section summary statement is an adequate close for the whole.

Throughout the book there are strong overtones about God's sovereignty—from God's miraculous inauguration of the church, to the Spirit empowered spread of the gospel, to the providential direction of the apostolic teams in their ministries. This strong theme is a continuation from Luke's Gospel. God had a sovereign plan which He was working out, and a grand part of this plan was the taking of the gospel to the Gentiles so He might redeem a people for Himself. Luke assures Theophilus and, by extension, all other Gentile readers that it was God's plan from the beginning to send the Jewish Messiah to be the Savior of all the world.

CHART 26 **Acts** ©2015 M. Scott Bashoor	***Purpose:*** Luke writes for Theophilus about the sovereign continuation of the Gospel ministry of Jesus as it developed in the ministries of Peter & Paul, showing how the gospel was intended for both Jews & Gentiles.	***Date:*** c. AD 61–63 ***Recipient:*** Theophilus (a Gentile convert of Paul?) ***Author:*** Luke, a ministry associate of Paul

INTRODUCTION: Hinge to the End Portion of Luke's Gospel 1:1–11	**MAIN BODY: Continuation of the Lord Jesus' Ministry thru the Apostles to Both Jews & Gentiles 1:12–28:31**					
	The Gospel Ministry Mostly to Jews thru the Leadership of Peter 1:12–12:24			**The Gospel Ministry Mostly to Gentiles thru the Leadership of Paul 12:25–28:31**		
Resumptive Preface 1:1–2 **Recounting of Resurrection Witnesses 1:3** **Jesus' Promise of the Coming of the Spirit 1:4–5** **Delay of the Earthly Kingdom, Soon Coming of the Spirit 1:6–8** **Recounting of the Ascension 1:9–11**	**Explosive Growth of the Gospel Ministry in Jerusalem 1:12–6:7** Prayerful Replacement of Judas & Waiting for the Spirit 1:12–26 Miraculous Empowerment by the Spirit 2:1–4:31 Faithful Persistence Despite Internal & External Challenges 4:32–6:6 Summary Statement 6:7	**Key Characters in the Further Spread of the Message 6:8–9:31** The Ministry & Martyrdom of Stephen 6:8–8:3 The Ministry of Philip in Samaria & Beyond 8:4–40 The Conversion of Saul, Future Apostle to the Gentiles 9:1–30 Summary Statement 9:31	**Climactic Report of the Apostolic Ministry under Peter 9:32–12:24** Geographic & Ethnic Expansion of Peter's Ministry 9:32–11:18 Authorized Establishment of a Mission Center in Antioch 11:19–30 Divine Protection & Validation of Peter's Ministry 12:1–23 Summary Statement 12:24	**Establishment of Paul's Apostolic Ministry to the Gentiles 12:25–16:5** The Spirit-Called First Missionary Journey 12:25–13:43 Jewish Rejection & Paul's Turning to the Gentiles 13:44–14:28 The Jerusalem Council's Commendation of Paul's Continued Ministry 15:1–16:4 Summary Statement 16:5	**Expansion of Paul's Apostolic Ministry to New Gentile Lands by Divine Direction 16:6–19:20** Divine Direction in Taking the Mission to Macedonia 16:6–40 Providential Direction in Moving from Macedonia to Greece 17:1–18:17 Providential Direction in the Ministry from Greece to Ephesus 18:18–19:19 Summary Statement 19:20	**Extension of Paul's Apostolic Ministry to Rome after Rejection in Jerusalem 19:21–28:31** Paul's Ministry Journey to Jerusalem & His Rejection 19:21–23:11 *Missions Work Continued with Prophetic Preparation for Rejection in Jerusalem 19:21–21:16* *Paul's Ministry in Jerusalem & the Jewish Rejection 21:17–23:11* Paul's Ministry as a Prisoner of Rome 23:12–28:29 *Paul's Ministry in Roman Imprisonment While in Palestine 23:12–26:32* *Paul's Ministry as a Prisoner en Route to Rome & upon Arrival 27:1–28:29* Summary Statement 28:30–31

CHART 27: Focus on Acts 1:12–6:7

INTRODUCTION, 1:1–11

MAIN BODY: CONTINUATION OF THE LORD JESUS' MINISTRY THRU THE APOSTLES TO BOTH JEWS & GENTILES, 1:12–28:31

THE GOSPEL MINISTRY MOSTLY TO JEWS THRU THE LEADERSHIP OF PETER, 1:12–12:24

Explosive Growth of the Gospel Ministry in Jerusalem, 1:12–6:7

Prayerful Replacement of Judas & Waiting for the Spirit 1:12–26

- The Setting: Gathered in the Upper Room 1:12–14
- Restoration of the Number of the 12 1:15–26
  - *Peter's Leadership in Replacing Judas 1:15*
  - *The Defection of Judas Explained as a Fulfillment 1:16–20a*
  - *The Selection of Matthias & His Installation 1:20b–26*

Miraculous Empowerment by the Spirit 2:1–4:31

At Pentecost 2:1–47

- The Spirit's Outpouring 2:1–13
  - *The Tongues of Fire & Speaking of Languages 2:1–4*
  - *The Response of the Crowd of Pilgrims 2:5–13*
- Peter's Sermon to the Pilgrim Worshipers 2:14–41
  - *The Spirit at Pentecost a Fulfillment of Scripture 2:14–21*
  - *Indictment for Crucifying the Promised Messiah 2:22–36*
  - *Call to Repentance & Faith Followed by Mass Conversions 2:37–41*
- The Glorious Aftermath of the Church's Fellowship 2:42–47

In the Temple 3:1–26

- Peter's Healing of the Crippled Beggar 3:1–10
- Peter's Sermon in Solomon's Portico 3:11–26
  - *The Healing as God's Validation of Jesus, Whom They had Disowned 3:11–16*
  - *Call to Repent & Receive Christ as the Fulfillment of the Prophetic Word & Initiator of Kingdom Blessings 3:17–26*

Amidst Persecution 4:1–31

- Peter & John before the Sanhedrin 4:1–22
  - *Arrest, Interrogation & Peter's Spirit Filled Response 4:1–12*
  - *The Council's Deliberation 4:13–17*
  - *The Order to Desist Defied by Peter & John 4:18–22*
- The Persecuted Church at Prayer 4:23–31
  - *Peter & John's Report 4:23*
  - *Prayer of Praise for God's Sovereign Works 4:24–28*
  - *Request for Vindication & Divine Empowerment 4:29–30*
  - *Divine Response to Prayer 4:31*

Faithful Persistence Despite Internal & External Challenges 4:32–6:6

- Challenges in Sharing Life Together 4:32–5:11
  - *The Freewill Sharing of Believers' Possessions & Barnabas's Great Example 4:32–37*
  - *The Deceitful Hypocrisy of Ananias & Sapphira 5:1–11*
- Powerful Ministry in the Temple & Opposition from the Temple Powers 5:12–42
  - *The Miraculous Ministry in Solomon's Portico Grows 5:12–16*
  - *Apostles Arrested, Miraculously Freed & Rearrested 5:17–26*
  - *Trial before the Sanhedrin: The Apostles' Boldness, Gamaliel's Wisdom & the Sentence of Flogging 5:27–40*
  - *The Apostles' Unhindered Joy & Ministry 5:41–42*
- The Challenge of Serving the Hellenist Women & the Introduction of the Seven 6:1–6
  - *The Problem of Neglected Widows at Meals 6:1–2*
  - *The Solution to Appoint Seven Spirit Filled Servants 6:3–6*

Summary Statement, 6:7

Key Characters in the Further Spread of the Message, 6:8–9:31

Climactic Report of the Apostolic Ministry Under Peter, 9:32–12:24

THE GOSPEL MINISTRY MOSTLY TO GENTILES THRU THE LEADERSHIP OF PAUL, 12:25–28:31

CHART 28: Focus on Acts 6:8–12:24

INTRODUCTION, 1:1–1 1

MAIN BODY: Continuation of the Lord Jesus' Ministry thru the Apostles to Both Jews & Gentiles, 1:12–28:31

The Gospel Ministry Mostly to Jews thru the Leadership of Peter, 1:12–12:24

Explosive Growth of the Gospel Ministry in Jerusalem, 1:12–6:7

Key Characters in the Further Spread of the Message 6:8–9:31				Climactic Report of the Apostolic Ministry Under Peter 9:32–12:24			
The Ministry & Martyrdom of Stephen 6:8–8:3	**The Ministry of Philip in Samaria & Beyond 8:4–40**	**The Conversion of Saul, Future Apostle to the Gentiles 9:1–30**	Summary Statement, 9:31	**Geographic & Ethnic Expansion of Peter's Ministry 9:32–11:18**	**Authorized Establish-ment of a Mission Center in Antioch 11:19–30**	**Divine Protection & Validation of Peter's Ministry 12:1–23**	Summary Statement, 12:24
Stephen's Arrest & Trial 6:8–7:1 *His Notable Ministry 6:8* *His Confounding of the Hellenist Synagogue Leaders 6:9–10* *False Allegations & Trial 6:11–7:1* Stephen's Speech before the Sanhedrin 7:2–53 *The Abrahamic Promises 7:2–8* *God's Deliverances thru Joseph & Moses 7:9–34* *Israel's Ancient & Ongoing Apostasy 7:35–50* *Their Rejection of Messiah 7:51–53* The Martyrdom of Stephen & the Introduction of Saul as a Persecutor 7:54–8:3	His Mission to Samaria 8:4–25 *Miraculous Witness 8:4–8* *Simon Magus's Profession of Faith 8:9–13* *The Spirit Conferred by Peter & John 8:14–17* *Confrontation of Simon's Evil Motives 8:18–25* Witness to the Ethiopian Eunuch 8:26–40 *Philip Directed to the Caravan in Gaza 8:26–29* *Philip's Witness & the Eunuch's Conversion 8:30–38* *Miraculous Ministry up the Coast 8:39–40*	Christ's Confrontation of Saul on the Road to Damascus 9:1–9 Christ's Revelation to Ananias of Saul's Call to Ministry to Gentiles & Jews 9:10–19a Saul's Ministry & Sufferings in Damascus 9:19b–25 Saul's Ministry & Sufferings in Jerusalem 9:26–30		Ministry in the Coastal Towns: Aeneas & Dorcas Healed 9:32–43 Ministry to the Gentile Cornelius in Caesarea 10:1–48 *Cornelius's Vision 10:1–8* *Peter's Vision 10:9–16* *Peter's Visit to Cornelius & the Sharing of Visions 10:17–33* *Peter's Sermon to Cornelius 10:34–43* *The Spirit's Impartial Coming upon the Gentiles 10:44–48* Report to Jerusalem 11:1–18 *Critical Reception at First 11:1–3* *Peter's Recounts the Vision & the Spirit's Work 11:4–17* *Joyful Reception of the News 11:18*	The Church Founded in Antioch 11:19–26 *Persecution Proliferates the Message 11:19* *Gentile Reception in Antioch 11:20–21* *Jerusalem Sends Barnabas to Confirm the Work 11:22–24* *Barnabas Brings Saul to Antioch for a Year of Ministry 11:25–26* Antioch's Love for Jerusalem Expressed in Famine Relief 11:27–30	Herod Agrippa's Persecutio n & the Death of James 12:1–5 Peter Miraculous -ly Delivered from Jail 12:6–19a Herod Smitten of God for Arrogance 12:19b–23	

The Gospel Ministry Mostly to Gentiles thru the Leadership of Paul, 12:25–28:31

<table>
<tr><th colspan="11">CHART 29: Focus on Acts 12:25–19:20</th></tr>
<tr><td rowspan="4">INTRODUCTION, 1:1–11</td><td colspan="10">MAIN BODY: CONTINUATION OF THE LORD JESUS' MINISTRY THRU THE APOSTLES TO BOTH JEWS & GENTILES, 1:12–28:31</td></tr>
<tr><td rowspan="3">THE GOSPEL MINISTRY MOSTLY TO JEWS THRU THE LEADERSHIP OF PETER, 1:12–12:24</td><td colspan="9">THE GOSPEL MINISTRY MOSTLY TO GENTILES THRU THE LEADERSHIP OF PAUL, 12:25–28:31</td></tr>
<tr><td colspan="4">Establishment of Paul's Apostolic Ministry to the Gentiles
12:25–16:5</td><td colspan="4">Expansion of Paul's Apostolic Ministry to New Gentile Lands by Divine Direction
16:6–19:20</td><td rowspan="2">Extension of Paul's Apostolic Ministry to Rome after Rejection in Jerusalem, 19:21–28:31</td></tr>
<tr>
<td>The Spirit-Called First Missionary Journey
12:25–13:41
The Spirit Sends Saul & Barnabas from Antioch
12:25–13:3
Ministry on Cyprus
13:4–12
Ministry to Jews, Greeks, the Magistrate & the Magician
13:4–8
Paul's Boldness & New Name
13:9–12
Ministry in Antioch of Pisidia
13:13–43
Ministry Setting & Circumstances
13:13–16a
Paul's Synagogue Sermon
13:16b–41
God's Ancient Promises to Israel
13:16b–25
Fulfillment thru Christ
13:26–37
Concluding Appeal
13:38–41</td>
<td>Jewish Rejection & Paul's Turning to the Gentiles
13:42–4:28
Aftermath of the Sermon
13:42–52
Paul's Turn to the Gentiles
13:42–47
Mixed Responses of Rejection & Joy
13:48–52
Jewish-led Rejection in Iconium
14:1–7
Gentile Ministry in Lystra
14:8–20a
Preaching & Healing
14:8–10
The Crowd's Adulation Turned to Rejection
14:11–20a
Ministry at Derbe
14:20b–21a
Follow Up in the Region & Return to Antioch to Report
14:21b–28</td>
<td>The Jerusalem Council's Commendation of Paul's Continued Ministry
15:1–16:5
Convening of the Council
15:1–29
Dissent over the Gentiles
15:1–2a
Antioch's Contingent Sent to Meet with the Apostles
15:2b–5
Peter's Defense of Paul
15:6–11
James' Proposed Resolution
15:12–21
Official Confirmation of Paul & Counsel for Jew-Gentile Relations
15:22–29
Aftermath of the Decision
15:30–16:4
Rejoicing & Rejuvenated Ministry in Antioch
15:30–35
New Partners in Paul's Mission Team to the Gentiles
15:36–16:4
Paul & Barnabas Part, Paul & Silas Set Out
15:36–41
Timothy Chosen by Paul & Circumcised for Tactical Reasons
16:1–5</td>
<td>Summary Statement, 16:5</td>
<td>Divine Direction in Taking the Mission to Macedonia
16:6–40
The Closed Door in Asia & the Call to Macedonia
16:6–10
Arrival & Ministry in Philippi
16:11–40
The Conversion of Lydia & Beginning of the Church
16:11–15
Deliverance of the Demon-possessed Girl
16:16–24
Imprison-ment of Paul & Silas
16:25–28
Conversion of the Jailor
16:29–34
Release of Paul & Silas
16:35–40</td>
<td>Providential Direction in Moving from Macedonia to Greece
17:1–18:17
Ministry in Thessalonica & Berea
17:1–15
Synagogue Teaching & the Jewish-led Riot
17:1–9
Reception in Berea Ended by Thessalonians
17:10–15
Ministry in Athens
17:16–34
In the Marketplace
17:16–21
At the Areopagus
17:22–31
The Mixed Result
17:32–34
Ministry in Corinth
18:1–17
Founding of the Church
18:1–8
An Assurance from Jesus & a Lengthy Stay
18:9–11
Trial before the Gallio
18:12–17</td>
<td>Providential Direction in the Ministry from Greece to Ephesus
18:18–19:19
Return to Antioch by Way of Ephesus
18:18–23
Ministry in Ephesus
18:24–19:22
Priscilla & Aquila Train Apollos for Strategic Ministry amongst Jews
18:24–28
The Spirit Descends on 12 Disciples of John
19:1–7
Summary of Paul's 2-Year Ministry
19:8–12
Paul's Countering of the 7 Sons of Sceva
19:13–19</td>
<td>Summary Statement, 19:20</td>
</tr>
</table>

CHART 30: Focus on Acts 19:21–23:10

INTRODUCTION, 1:1–1:1

MAIN BODY: CONTINUATION OF THE LORD JESUS' MINISTRY THRU THE APOSTLES TO BOTH JEWS & GENTILES, 1:12–28:31

THE GOSPEL MINISTRY MOSTLY TO JEWS THRU THE LEADERSHIP OF PETER, 1:12–12:24

THE GOSPEL MINISTRY MOSTLY TO GENTILES THRU THE LEADERSHIP OF PAUL, 12:25–28:31

Establishment of Paul's Apostolic Ministry to the Gentiles, 12:25–16:5

Expansion of Paul's Apostolic Ministry to New Gentile Lands by Divine Direction, 16:6–19:20

Extension of Paul's Apostolic Ministry to Rome after Rejection in Jerusalem 19:21–28:31

Paul's Ministry Journey to Jerusalem & His Rejection 19:21–23:11

Missions Work Continued with Prophetic Preparation for Rejection in Jerusalem 19:21–21:16		Paul's Ministry in Jerusalem & the Jewish Rejection 21:17–23:11	
Forced Departure from Ephesus 19:21–41	**Roundabout Route to Jerusalem 20:1–21:16**	**Paul's Reception & the Temple Riot 21:17–40**	**Paul's Testimony Before the Crowd & the Sanhedrin 21:37–23:11**
Paul's Intention to go to Jerusalem 19:21–22 The Riot in Ephesus 19:23–41 *The Instigation by Demetrius, the Idol Craftsman 19:23–27* *The Tumult in the Theater 19:28–34* *The City Clerk's Intervention 19:35–41*	Follow-up Visit to Macedonia & Achaia 20:1–6 The Raising of Eutychus at Troas 20:7–12 Travel to Miletus & Farwell to the Ephesian Elders 20:13–38 *The Passage to Miletus & the Rush to Jerusalem 20:13–16* *The Long Farewell 20:17–38* Their Shared Past & Paul's Uncertain Future 20:17–27 Warnings about Their Future, Admonitions & Farewell Blessings 20:28–38 The Final Passage to Jerusalem 21:1–16 *Passage to Tyre & Prophetic Warnings 21:1–21:6* *Journey to Caesarea & the Prophetic Warning of Agabus 21:7–16*	Paul with the Church 21:17–26 *The Church's Warm Reception 21:17–20a* *The Church's Concern Over Jew-Gentile Controversies & Conspiracy Theories 21:20b–22* *The Decision for Paul to Visit the Temple with Other Christians Fulfilling Vows 21:23–26* Paul's Arrival at the Temple & the Ensuing Riot 21:27–36 *The False Accusation of Paul's Sacrilege & Their Vicious Attack 21:27–30* *The Intervention of the Roman Commander & Paul's Arrest 21:31–36*	Paul's Testimony to the Crowd 21:37–22:21 *Request to Address the Crowd 21:37–40* *Testimony of His Past Life 22:1–5* *Recounting of His Conversion 22:6–16* *Paul's Heavenly Commission to the Gentiles 22:17–21* The Attempt to Torture Paul & the Advantage of His Citizenship 22:22–29 Paul's Testimony before the Sanhedrin 22:30–23:11 *The Setting: The Next Day 22:30* *Paul's Claim of Innocence & the Violent Argument 23:1–5* *Paul's Pitting of the Parties Against Each Other 23:6–9* *Paul Taken into Roman Custody & Jesus' Assurance 23:10–11*

Paul's Ministry as a Prisoner in Route to Rome, 23:12–28:11

Summary Statement, 28:30–31

CHART 31: Focus on Acts 23:11–28:31

INTRODUCTION, 1:1–11

MAIN BODY: CONTINUATION OF THE LORD JESUS' MINISTRY THRU THE APOSTLES TO BOTH JEWS & GENTILES, 1:12–28:31

THE GOSPEL MINISTRY MOSTLY TO JEWS THRU THE LEADERSHIP OF PETER, 1:12–12:24

THE GOSPEL MINISTRY MOSTLY TO GENTILES THRU THE LEADERSHIP OF PAUL, 12:25–28:31

Establishment of Paul's Apostolic Ministry to the Gentiles, 12:25–16:5

Expansion of Paul's Apostolic Ministry to New Gentile Lands by Divine Direction, 16:6–19:20

Extension of Paul's Apostolic Ministry to Rome after Rejection in Jerusalem 19:21–28:31

Paul's Ministry Journey to Jerusalem & His Rejection, 19:21–23:10

Paul's Ministry as a Prisoner of Rome 23:12–28:11

Paul's Ministry in Roman Imprisonment While in Palestine 23:12–26:32		**Paul's Ministry as a Prisoner in Route to Rome & upon Arrival 27:1–28:29**	
Paul before Felix & Festus 23:12–25:12	**Paul before Herod Agrippa 25:13–26:32**	**Paul's Ministry in Route to Rome 27:1–28:16**	**Paul's Ministry in Prison in Rome 28:17–28 [29]**
The Jerusalem Plot to Assassinate Paul 23:12–22 Paul Evacuated to Caesarea 23:23–35 *Preparations for Transport & the Commander's Letter to Felix 23:23–30* *Armed Transport to Caesarea 23:31–35* The Hearing before Felix 24:1–27 *The Opening Accusation 24:1–9* *Paul's Defense 24:10–21* *Felix's 2 Years of Indecision 24:22–27* The Case under Festus 25:1–12 *The Jews Press for Action 25:1–5* *Paul Appeals to Caesar 25:6–12*	Festus' Discussion of the Case with Agrippa 25:13–22 The Hearing before Agrippa 25:23–26:32 *Festus & Felix's Preliminary Discussion 25:23–27* *Paul's Defense 26:1–23* Cordial Introduction 26:1–3 His Former Life in Judaism 26:4–11 His Conversion & Commissioning by Christ 26:12–18 Recounting of His Mission Work 26:19–23 *Festus' Incredulousness 26:24* *Paul's Direct Appeal to Agrippa 26:25–29* *The Informal Declaration of Innocence 26:30–32*	Voyage from Caesarea to Crete & Paul's Prophetic Warning of Peril 27:1–12 The Great Storm & Island Shipwreck 27:13–44 *The Ship's Battle with a Northeastern 27:13–20* *Paul's Prophetic Assurance from Jesus 27:21–26* *Paul's Insightful Counsel to Sailors & Crew 27:27–38* *Mass Survival of the Island Shipwreck 27:39–44* The Stay on Malta 28:1–10 *Paul's Miraculous Survival of a Viper Bite 28:1–6* *Healing Ministry at the House of Publius 28:7–10* The Final Leg to Rome & the Encouragement of Brothers Met on the Way 28:11–16	Paul's Initial Witness & Defense to Roman Jews 28:17–22 Further Ministry to Jews with Mixed Results 28:23–24 Isaiah's Indictment against Unbelieving Jews Fulfilled Again 28:25–28 [29]

Summary Statement, 28:30–31

THE EPISTLE TO THE ROMANS

Written in the mid-50s from Corinth to the church at Rome, Paul's epistle to the Romans is his longest letter and *magum opus*. He'd heard reports that this church of Jews and Gentiles was struggling in its unity. Paul had been correcting disunity in Corinth for some time, and he doubtless wanted to stem similar carnality in Rome. In Romans, therefore, Paul expounds to Jewish and Gentile Christians their common bond in the gospel, urging them to accept one another based on their shared experience of saving faith in Christ.

The problems in Rome (see chap. 12–15) were fallouts from a previous period of oppression. In AD 49 Emperor Claudius expelled all Jews from Rome, including Jewish Christians (Acts 18:2). This left the church as an entirely Gentile congregation until Jews returned in AD 54 when Nero reversed Claudius' decree. The church again became ethnically mixed, but there were tensions between the groups over matters of conscience and liberty. Paul writes in an alternating style, sometimes addressing Jews, sometimes addressing Gentiles, and sometimes both. He repeatedly stresses the common problems they faced as sinners and the common solution they have through the gospel of Christ—which saves both Jew and Gentile (1:16).

There is some debate as to Paul's primary purpose in writing. Is it an evangelistic strategy to penetrate the heart of the empire (1:15)? Is it an apologetic for the Christian faith (1:16)? Is it a preparatory letter for Paul's planned mission trip to the far West (15:23–24)? Or is it primarily a pastoral letter, addressing a budding problem in a key church (15:1–2)? Perhaps all of these are at play, but the last two are most likely dominant. The Roman church was a strategic congregation with mature workers (15:14), and Paul would need the support of Rome if he was going to minister in the far West. For this to occur, the saints at Rome needed to understand the gospel's universality and Paul's mission to the Gentiles.

The outlines follow a traditional understanding of Paul's argument. In the introduction (1:1–17), Paul graciously greets his readers, explains his plan to visit them, and shares the theme of his letter: the salvation of Jew and Gentile by faith in the gospel. The body of the letter focuses chiefly on doctrinal concerns (1:18–11:36), particularly how Jews and Gentiles share the same hope in the gospel. Both share a common problem in their natural depravity and the judgment it merits. There is a single solution for this problem in the righteousness of Christ who alone can justify sinners. Salvation leads all believers into a common life of holiness, whether they are Jews or Gentiles. The seeming problem of God's setting Israel aside is addressed at length (chap. 9–11). Israel's rejection is only for a time to allow a great ingathering of Gentiles before a final generation of Jews are saved. Thus, God remains faithful to His promises to national Israel.

Throughout chapters 12–15, Paul addresses practical concerns of Jews and Gentiles living in Christian unity. They need renewed minds to enable them to live together in love, to use their gifts responsibly, and to be at peace with one another and the world around them.

In the conclusion to the letter (15:14–16:27), Paul explains his ministry model of forging into new territory and how he plans to do mission work as far west as Spain. For that he requests the support of this important church before closing with extensive greetings from fellow saints who were also saved through the grace of Jesus.

CHART 32 Romans ©2015 M. Scott Bashoor	***Purpose***: Paul expounds the gospel to Gentile & Jewish Christians to counsel them to accept one another since God accepted them based on the righteousness they'd received by faith in Christ.	***Date:*** *c.* AD 56 during Paul's 3rd missionary journey ***Recipients:*** Jew & Gentile Christians in Rome ***Origination:*** Written by Paul while in Corinth

INTRODUCTION 1:1–17	**BODY OF THE LETTER 1:18–15:13**							**CONCLUSION 15:14–16:27**	
Greetings of Grace 1:1–7 Paul's Plan to Visit 1:8–15 Theme of the Book: Salvation by Faith for Jew & Gentile 1:16–17	**DOCTRINAL CONCERNS: The Gospel as the Hope of Jews & Gentiles 1:18–11:36**				**PRACTICAL CONCERNS: The Church Together with Jews & Gentiles 12:1–15:13**			**Paul's Method for Ministry & Future Gospel Mission 15:14–33**	**Closing Commendations, Greetings, & Counsel 16:1–27**
	***A Common Problem:* Depravity & Judgment 1:18–3:20**	***A Single Solution:* Righteousness thru God's Justification 3:21–5:21**	***A Shared Holiness:* Sanctification for Jew & Gentile 6:1–8:39**	***The Sovereign Plan:* Israel in God's Program 9:1–11:36**	***Transition:* New Lives, Renewed Minds 12:1–2**	***Together in Love:* Hallmarks of Christian Community 12:3–13:14**	***Sorting out Differences:* Deferring on Lesser Matters of Conscience 14:1–15:13**		
	Gentiles Lost in Sin 1:18–32 Jews Lost in Sin 2:1–3:8 All Lost in Sin 3:9–20	Righteousness thru Christ's Sacrifice for Jew and Gentile 3:21–31 Abraham, Father to Both Jew & Gentile Believers 4:1–25 Hope for All Only in Christ 5:1–21	Grace Overpowers Sin 6:1–23 United to Christ by Grace, Not Law 7:1–6 The Struggle Involving Sin & Law 7:7–25 Life in the Spirit 8:1–30 Celebration of Hope 8:31–39	Paul's Burden for Lost Israel 9:1–5 Israel Hardened, Gentiles Softened 9:6–29 Israel's Rejection of The Gospel 9:30–10:21 Israel to One Day be Saved & Restored 11:1–32 Celebrating Sovereignty 11:33–36	Gospel Mercies Call for Dedication of Life & Renewal of the Mind 12:1–2	Using Gifts for the Body 12:3–8 Living at Peace with Each Other 12:9–13 Living at Peace in Society 12:14–13:7 Loving Others & Living Right 13:8–14	Differences over Jewish Diet & Calendar Keeping 14:1–12 Gentiles Causing Jews to Stumble 14:13–23 Gentiles to Show Loving Deference to Jews 15:1–6 Jews & Gentiles to Live in Unity 15:7–13	Exhorting Established Churches, Establishing New Territory Churches 15:14–21 Plans to Visit Rome & Expand the Ministry to the West 15:22–33	Commendations & Greetings 16:1–16 Warning Regarding False Brethren 16:17–20 Farewells & Final Prayer 16:21–27

CHART 33: Focus on Romans 1:18–5:21

INTRODUCTION, 1:1–17

BODY OF THE LETTER, 1:18–15:13

DOCTRINAL CONCERNS: The Gospel as the Hope of Jews & Gentiles, 1:18–11:36

***A Common Problem:* Depravity & Judgment 1:18–3:20**			***A Single Solution:* Righteousness thru God's Justification 3:21–5:21**		
Gentiles Lost in Sin 1:18–32	**Jews Lost in Sin 2:1–3:8**	**All Lost in Sin 3:9–20**	**Righteousness thru Christ's Sacrifice for Jew & Gentile 3:21–31**	**Abraham, Father to Both Jew & Gentile Believers 4:1–25**	**Hope for All Only in Christ 5:1–21**
The Gentiles' Abandonment of God 1:18–23 *The Knowledge of God Suppressed by Sinful Man* *1:18–21* *The Knowledge of God Exchanged for Corruptible Substitutes* *1:22–23* God's Wrath of Abandonment 1:24–32 *Abandonment to Sinful Desires* *1:24–27* *Abandonment to Depravity of Mind* *1:28–32*	God's Impartial Judgment of the Jews 2:1–16 *The Inexcusable Wickedness of Self-Righteousness* *2:1–3* *Judgment according to One's Works* *2:4–11* *Judgment according to the Law of God* *2:12–16* Uncircumcised Hearts 2:17–29 *Paul's Interrogation of a Self-righteous Jew* *2:17–24* *The Need for Circumcision of the Heart* *2:25–29* Judgment in Accord with God's Faithfulness 3:1–8 *God's Faithfulness Despite Israel's Unbelief* *3:1–4* *God's Faithfulness Undiminished by Judgment* *3:5–8*	Jews No Better 3:9 All Indicted by Scripture 3:10–18 *Psalms 14:1-3; 53:1–3* *3:10–12* *Psalm 5:9* *3:13a* *Psalm 140:3* *3:13b* *Psalm 10:7* *3:14* *Isaiah 59:7-8* *3:15–17* *Psalm 36:1* *3:18* All Accountable to God 3:19–20	Righteousness thru Christ's Sacrifice 3:21–26 *Righteousness Obtainable by Sinful Jews & Gentiles Only Thru Christ* *3:21–23* *A Public Demonstrat-ion of God's Righteousness* *3:24–25* Righteousness by Faith for Jew & Gentile 3:27–31 *The Nullification of Pride in Law Keeping* *3:27–28* *The Justification of All Believers by Faith* *3:29-30* *The Establishment of the Law's Claims* *3:31*	Abraham Not Justified by Works 4:1–8 *The Record of Abraham's Faith* *4:1–3* *The Credit of Righteousness Thru Faith* *4:4–8* Justification without Circumcision 4:9–12 *Abraham Justified Before His Circumcision* *4:9–11a* *Abraham, the Faither of Uncircmcised Believers* *4:11b–12* Justification apart from the Law 4:13–16 Abraham, the Father of All Believers 4:17–25 *Abraham's Faith in the Seemingly Impossible Promise* *3:17–22* *Encouragement to All Believers from Abraham's Justification* *3:23–25*	Peace with God & Hope in Christ 5:1–11 *Peace with God thru Justification in Christ* *5:1–2a* *Eschatological Hope in the Midst of Many Present Sufferings* *5:2b–5* *Christ's Help of Helpless Sinners* *5:6–8* *Reconciliation of Sinners to God* *5:9–11* Christ, the Conqueror of Adam's Sin 5:12–19 *The Reign of Death Since Adam's Sin* *5:12–14* *The Reign of Life Since Christ's Sacriice* *5:15–19* The Role of the Law to Magnify Sin & Grace 5:20–21

***A Shared Holiness:* Sanctification for Jew & Gentile, 6:1–8:39**

***The Sovereign Plan:* Israel in God's Program, 9:1–11:36**

PRACTICAL CONCERNS: The Church Together with Jews & Gentiles, 12:1–15:13

CONCLUSION, 15:14–16:27

CHART 34: Focus on Romans 6:1–11:36

INTRODUCTION, 1:1–17

BODY OF THE LETTER, 1:18–15:13

DOCTRINAL CONCERNS: The Gospel as the Hope of Jews & Gentiles, 1:18–11:36

A Common Problem: Depravity & Judgment, 1:18–3:20

A Single Solution: Righteousness thru God's Justification, 3:21–5:21

A Shared Holiness: **Sanctification for Jew & Gentile 6:1–8:39**					***The Sovereign Plan:*** **Israel in God's Program 9:1–11:36**				
Grace Over-powers Sin 6:1–23	**Unit-ed to Christ thru Grace Not Law 7:1–6**	**The Struggle Involving Sin & Law 7:7–25**	**Life in the Spirit 8:1–30**	**Cele-bration of Christ-ian Hope 8:31–39**	**Paul's Burden for Priv-ileged Israel 9:1–5**	**Israel Hardened; Gentiles Softened 9:6–29**	**Israel's Rejection of The Gospel 9:30–10:21**	**Israel to One Day be Saved & Restored 11:1–32**	**Celebra-tion of God's Sover-eignty 11:33–36**
Dead to Sin, Alive to God 6:1–14 *United with Christ's Death & Dead to Sin 6:1–7* *United with Christ's Life & Alive to Right-eousness 6:8–14* Freed from Sin, Enslaved to Right-eousness 6:15–23 *The Inevi-tability of Enslave-ment 6:15–19* *The Sur-passing Benefits of Slavery to Right-eousness 6:20–23*	The Anal-ogy of Wi-dow-hood 7:1–3 The Law's Death & the Be-lieve-er's Free-dom in Christ 7:4-6	Conviction of Sin thru the Law 7:7–12 *Paul's Conviction under the 10th command-ment 7:7–11* *Summary of the Law's Holiness 7:12* The Battle with Sin Exposed by the Law 7:13–25 *The Law's Exposure of Sin 7:13* *The Battle with Indwelling Sin 7:14–20* *The Battle of Indwelling Principles 7:21–25*	Freedom from Sin by the Spirit 8:1–13 *Free from Sin's Judgment & Bondage 8:1–4a* *Free from the Flesh to Live by the Spirit 8:4b–8* *The Condition of New Life in the Spirit 8:8–13* Adoption as Sons by the Spirit 8:14–17 Glory to Come thru the Spirit 8:18–30 *Glory to Surpass Present Suffering 8:18–25* *The Spirit's Help to the Elect in Present Sufferings 8:26–30*	Rhetor-ical Quest-ions about Salvat-ion 8:31–37 Climac-tic Cele-bration of God's Insep-arable Love 8:38–39	His Grief over Their Lost Estate 9:1-3 His Re-count-ing of their Spiritual Heritage 9:4-5	Not All Israel is the True Israel 9:6–13 *Not All Ethnic Jews are Spiritual Jews 9:6* *Not all Descendants of Abraham Inherited the Promises 9:7–12* God's Sovereignty in Salvation 9:14–29 *Israel's Unbelief Not a Sign of God's Injustice 9:14* *God's Prerogative in Mercy 9:15–18* *The Potter's Freedom 9:19–24* *Prophecies of Israel's Unbelief 9:25–29*	Israel's Loss of Real Righteousness 9:30–10:4 *Israel's Stumbling Over Christ 9:30–33* *Israel's Salvation Only thru Christ 10:1–4* Israel's Need for Gospel Righteousness 10:5–13 *The Nearness of Salvation in Christ 10:5–10* *The Promise of Salvation to All Who Believe 10:11–13* Israel's Obligation to Hear 10:14–21 *The Proclamation in All the World 10:14–18* *Israel's Ongoing Unbelief 10:19–21*	An Elect Remnant Today 11:1–10 *God's Preservation of a Remnant throughout History 11:1–6* *The Few Chosen & Many Forsaken 11:7–10* God's Global Purpose in Israel's Rejection 11:11–24 *The Ingathering of Gentiles & the Jealousy of the Jews 11:11–16* *The In-grafting of Gentiles & Eventual Regrafting of Jews 11:17–24* A Generat-ion of Israel to be Saved 11:25–32	God's Unfath-onable Wisdom 11:33 God's Incom-parable Mind 11:34 God's Indebt-edness to No One 11:35 God's Govern-ance of All Things 11:36

PRACTICAL CONCERNS: The Church Together with Jews & Gentiles, 12:1–15:13

CONCLUSION, 15:14–16:27

CHART 35: Focus on Romans 12:1–16:27

INTRODUCTION, 1:1–17

DOCTRINAL CONCERNS: The Gospel as the Hope of Jews & Gentiles, 1:18–11:36

BODY OF THE LETTER 1:18–15:13			CONCLUSION 15:14–16:27	
PRACTICAL CONCERNS: The Church Together with Jews & Gentiles 12:1–15:13			**Paul's Method for Ministry & Future Gospel Mission 15:14–33**	**Closing Commendations, Greetings & Counsel 16:1–27**
Transition: **New Lives, Renewed Minds 12:1–2**	***Together in Love:*** **Hallmarks of Christian Community 12:3–13:14**	***Sorting out Differences:*** **Deferring on Lesser Matters of Conscience 14:1–15:13**		
The Call to Dedication Based on Gospel Mercies 12:1 **The Call to Mind Renewal for Spiritual Transfor-mation 12:2**	**Using Gifts for the Body 12:3–8** **Living at Peace with Each Other 12:9–13** **Living at Peace in Society 12:14–13:7** Loving your Enemies, Supporting One Another 12:14–21 Submitting to Ordained Authorities 13:1–7 **Loving Others & Living Right 13:8–14** Love Fulfills the Law 13:8–10 Living Right in God's Light 13:11–14	**Differences over Jewish Diet & Calendar Keeping 14:1–12** Accepting One Another Despite Religious Diets & Dates 14:1–6 Living for Others, Not Oneself 14:7–9 Recognizing God as the Ultimate Judge 14:10–12 **Gentiles Causing Jews to Stumble 14:13–23** Avoiding Stumbling Blocks 14:13 Being Informed But Sensative 14:14–18 Promoting Unity & Preserving Conscience 14:19–23 **Gentiles to Show Loving Deference to Jews 15:1–6** **Jew & Gentile to Live in Unity 15:7–13**	**Exhorting Established Churches & Establishing New Territory Churches 15:14–21** Exhorting Established Churches 15:14–15 Special Mission to the Gentiles 15:16–19 Method of Establishing Churches without Competition 15:20–21 **Plans to Visit Rome & Expand the Ministry to the West 15:22–33** The Romans' Help Needed for the New Western Campaign 15:22–24 The Jerusalem Fund to be Delivered First 15:25–29 Request for Prayers, & Paul's Prayer of Blessings 15:30–33	**Commendations & Greetings 16:1–16** Commendation of Phoebe 16:1–2 Greetings to Precious Coworkers 16:3–16 **Warning Regarding False Brethren 16:17–20** **Farewells & Final Prayer 16:21–27** Farewell Greetings from Paul's Associates 16:21–23 [24] Closing Doxology 16:25–27

Paul's two letters to the Corinthians, written in AD 56, address dire concerns he had with a large church with larger problems. This troubled church received more correspondence from Paul than any other, comprising 30% of his inspired writings.

Occasioning this correspondence is conflict, misunderstanding, and carnality on the part of the Corinthian saints. Historically, the church at Corinth was founded by the Apostle around AD 50. He spent an unprecedented 18 months there, laboring to establish the church before cycling back East. Years later Paul received troubling reports, and in early AD 56 he received a letter with questions from the church itself. It appears that Paul wrote two other letters to them (1 Cor 5:9–13; 2 Cor 2:4) before and between the two inspired letters in the NT. Moreover, he made a painful visit to confront problems head-on before writing 2 Corinthians (2 Cor 2:1).

PAUL'S INTERACTIONS WITH THE CORINTHIANS								
Fall 50–Spring 52	**c. 55**	**Spring 56**	**Spring 56**	**Spring 56**	**Spring 56**	**Summer 56**	**Summer or Fall 56**	**Winter 56–57**
Church Founded	Bad Reports Prompt Paul's Initial Letter	Church Replies & Sends Questions	Paul Writes 1 Cor.	Paul's Emergency Visit	Paul's Harsh Letter	Paul's Anxious Summer in Troas & Macedonia	Paul Writes 2 Cor.	Paul's Final Visit

In **First Corinthians** Paul responds to reports and questions from Corinth by applying gospel truths to problems threatening their unity and holiness. His approach is different from most of his letters in that he does not frontload this epistle with doctrinal teaching followed by prolonged, practical application. Instead, he alternates between doctrinal and practical discussions, perhaps because the immature members could not yet profit as much from extended exposition.

First Corinthians opens with Paul's introductory greetings of grace. In the first half of the letter, he addresses his concerns based on reports about problems in Corinth. Throughout the first six chapters, he tackles the rather visible divisions in the church which were based largely on misconceptions about the gospel's public reception and solid Christian ministry. Moreover, Paul addresses the church's massive disorder evidenced in their lack of basic church discipline, their shameful dragging of one another into court, and their toleration of gross immorality. In the latter half of the letter, from chapters seven though fifteen, Paul answers questions the Corinthians posed about marriage, about food purchased from pagan temples, and issues in their public worship. He also addresses the use of spiritual gifts, and, last but not least, the nature of Christian resurrection. In the letter's conclusion, he provides instructions about an important collection for the Jerusalem church and informs them of his plans to visit soon.

Second Corinthians was necessitated in part because Paul could not keep his travel itinerary. In his absence, a malicious group attacked his apostolic credentials, requiring him to tackle their misunderstandings about true gospel ministry. He begins by greeting them with grace and celebrating God's abounding comfort. Throughout the first half of the letter, he answers concerns about his delay. Critics argued Paul was afraid to come back, but he explains his heart and the unforeseen turn of events in his schedule. While discussing his trials, the apostle digresses at length on the glories of the gospel ministry before explaining how his itinerary problems resolved. He also directs that they resume their collection for the Jerusalem fund before responding to accusations by certain rebellious leaders. Paul uncomfortably defends his apostolic ministry before warning of an upcoming visit in which he will confront the unrepentant element of false teachers before concluding with firm instructions and gracious prayer.

CHART 36 1 Corinthians ©2015 M. Scott Bashoor	***Purpose:*** Paul responds to reports and questions from Corinth by applying gospel truths to threats against the unity and holiness to their church.	***Date:*** Spring AD 56, in 3rd missionary journey ***Recipients:*** The Gentile church at Corinth ***Origination:*** During Paul's stay in Ephesus

INTRO-DUCTION 1:1–9	**BODY OF THE LETTER 1:10–15:58**							**CON-CLUSION 16:1–24**
	PAUL ADDRESSES HIS CONCERNS BASED ON REPORTS RECEIVED 1:10–6:20		**PAUL ANSWERS THE CORINTHIANS' QUESTIONS THEY'VE WRITTEN TO HIM 7:1–15:58**					
Initial Greetings 1:1–3 **Prayerful Thanks-giving 1:4–9**	**Major Divisions in the Church 1:10–4:21** The Visibility of Divisions 1:10–17 Divisive Misconcept-ions about the Gospel Message 1:18–3:4 Divisive Misconcept-ions about the Gospel Ministry 3:5–4:21	**Massive Disorder in the Church 5:1–6:20** The Utter Lack of Church Discipline 5:1–13 The Tragedy of Christian Lawsuits 6:1–11 The Toleration of Immorality 6:12–20	**Regarding Relationships 7:1–40** Counsel Regarding Marriage 7:1–24 Counsel Regarding Fathers and Virgin Daughters 7:25–40	**Regarding Foods & Idol Worship 8:1–11:1** Love Must Guide Our Choices 8:1–13 Paul's Use of Freedom in Ministry 9:1–27 Avoid All Idolatry 10:1–11:1	**Regarding the Public Assembly 11:2–34** Women's Immodest Attire 11:2–16 Problems at Lord's Table 11:17–34	**Regarding Spiritual Gifts in the Church 12:1–14:40** The Unity & Diversity of Gifts 12:1–31 The More Excellent Way of Love 13:1–13 The Need for Intelligibility & Order 14:1–40	**Regarding Christ's & the Christian's Resurrection 15:1–58** The Gospel Message & Christian Hope 15:1–19 The Order of Resurrection Events Past & Future 15:20–28 Resurrection Motivates the Gospel Ministry 15:29–34 The Nature of the Resurrection Body 15:35–49 The Basis of Christian Confidence & Service 15:50–58	**Instruct-ions Regarding Jerusalem Collection 16:1–9** Collect-ions to be Saved Weekly 16:1–4 Paul's Itinerary 16:5–9 **Ministers & Messen-gers Traveling; Acknow-ledgments 16:10–19** **Greetings, A Warning, & A Prayer of Blessing 16:20–24**

CHART 37: Focus on 1 Corinthians 1:10–6:20

INTRODUCTION, 1:1–9

BODY OF THE LETTER, 1:10–15:58

PAUL ADDRESSES HIS CONCERNS BASED ON REPORTS RECEIVED, 1:10–6:20

Major Divisions in the Church 1:10–4:21			**Massive Disorder in the Church 5:1–6:20**		
Visibility of Divisions 1:10–17	**Misconceptions about the Gospel Message 1:18–3:4**	**Misconceptions about the Gospel Ministry 3:5–4:21**	**The Utter Lack of Church Discipline 5:1–13**	**The Tragedy of Christian Lawsuits 6:1–11**	**The Toleration of Immorality 6:12–20**
Exhortation to Unity 1:10 Report from Chloe's People about Divisions 1:11–12 The Folly of Partisan Division in Christ 1:13–17	The Gospel Contrary to Human Wisdom 1:18–2:5 *The Folly of the Cross 1:18–25* *The Folly of the Corinthians' Election 1:26–31* *The Folly of Paul's Preaching 2:1–5* The Gospel Conveys the Wisdom of God 2:6–3:4 *The Spirit Reveals God's Gospel Wisdom 2:6–16* *The Carnal Understanding of the Corinthians 3:1–4*	Servant Workers in God's Field 3:5–9a Builders of God's House 3:9b–17 *The Imagery Amplified 3:9b–11* *Charge to Prepare for Accounting 3:12–17* Christ is Head of All His Workers 3:18–23 Proper Regard for Apostles 4:1–21 *Servants Judged by God Alone 4:1–5* *Sacrificial Marks of True Apostles 4:6–13* *Appeal to Imitate Paul's Attitude 4:14–21*	The Need to Expel the Notorious, Incestuous Man 5:1–5 Paul's Argument for Expulsion: The Analogy of Passover 5:6–8 Clarification on Interaction with Immoral People 5:9–13 *Not Isolation from Outsiders 5:9–10* *But Separation from Unrepentant Brothers 5:11–13*	Shame on the Church for its Christians' Litigation 6:1–6 Shame on the Litigant for Going Before the Courts 6:7 Warning to Wrongdoers of God's Judgment 6:8–10 Encouragement from the Gospel to Pursue Holiness 6:11	Bodily Appetites Do Not Justify Immorality 6:12–13a A Theology of the Body & Sexual Purity 6:13b–17 The Command to Flee Immorality and Its Rationale 6:18–20 *The Admonition 6:18a* *The Unique Defilement of Immorality 6:18b–20*

PAUL ANSWERS THE QUESTIONS THEY HAVE WRITTEN TO HIM, 7:1–15:58

CONCLUSION, 16:1–24

CHART 38: Focus on 1 Corinthians 7:1–15:58

INTRODUCTION, 1:1–9

BODY OF THE LETTER, 1:10–15:58

PAUL ADDRESSES HIS CONCERNS BASED ON REPORTS RECEIVED, 1:10–6:20

PAUL ANSWERS THE CORINTHIANS' QUESTIONS WHICH THEY'VE WRITTEN TO HIM 7:1–15:58

Regarding Relationships 7:1–40	Regarding Foods & Idol Worship 8:1–11:1	Regarding the Public Assembly 11:2–34	Regarding Spiritual Gifts in the Church 12:1–14:40			Regarding the Christian's Resurrection 15:1–58
			Unity & Diversity of Gifts 12:1–31	**The More Excellent Way of Love 13:1–13**	**The Need for Intel-ligibility & Order 14:1–40**	
Counsel on Marriage 7:1–24 *Marital Intimacy 7:1–5* *Celibacy Versus Marriage 7:6–9* *Divorce for Christians 7:10–16* *"Stay as You Are" 7:17–24* Counsel on Virgins & Marriage 7:25–38 *Celibacy Good but Not Required 7:25–28* *Benefits of Celibacy 7:29–38* Counsel on Widows & Remarriage 7:39–40	Love Must Guide Our Choices 8:1–13 *Proper Knowledge without Love 8:1–6* *The Stumbling Block of Pagan Festivals 8:7–13* Paul's Use of Freedom 9:1–27 *Apostolic Right to Support 9:1–14* *Refusal of Support 9:15–23* *Illustration of Self-Discipline 9:24–27* Avoid All Idolatry 10:1–11:1 *Lessons from OT Israel 10:1–13* *Communion with Christ & Demons 10:14–22* *About Temple Meat 10:23–11:1*	Women's Immodest Attire 11:2–16 *Appeal to a Sense of Shame 11:2–6* *Appeal to Order of Creation 11:7–13* *Appeal to a Propriety 11:14–16* Problems at the Lord's Table 11:17–34 *The Discommun-ion of the Poor 11:17–22* *The Sacredness of Communion 11:23–26* *Discerning the Body 11:27–32* *Sharing the Simple Meal 11:33–34*	*The Foundation of Jesus' Lordship 12:1–3* *The Trinity as a Model of Variety & Unity 12:4–6* *One Spirit Distributes Different Gifts 12:7–11* *The Diversity & Unity of the Body 12:12–26* *The Order of Gifts in the Body 12:27–31*	*The Supreme Necessity of Love 13:1–3* *The Actions of Christian Love 13:4–7* *The Perma-nence of Love Contrasted with Spiritual Gifts 13:8–13*	*Superiority of Prophecy to Tongues 14:1–5* *Examples of Useless Sounds 14:6–12* *The Use of the Mind in Worship 14:13–19* *Need for Maturity & Under-standing 14:20–25* *Spiritual Controls on Tongue Speaking & Prophesy-ing 14:26–33* *Women to be Silent in the Assembly 14:34–35* *Final Charge to Submit to Paul's Instruction 14:36–40*	The Gospel Message & Christian Hope 15:1–19 *Christ's Resurrection Fundamental to the Gospel 15:1–11* *The Christian Hopeless without Resurrection 15:12–19* The Order of Resurrection Events Past and Future 15:20–28 Relevance of Resurrection to Gospel Ministry 15:29–34 The Nature of the Resurrection Body 15:35–49 *Illustrated by Various Seeds & Bodies 15:35–44* *A Body Like Christ's Heavenly Body 15:45–49* The Basis of Christian Confidence & Service 15:50–58

CONCLUSION, 16:1–24

CHART 39 2 Corinthians ©2015 M. Scott Bashoor	***Purpose:*** Paul responds again to reports from Corinth, tackling their misunderstanding of true gospel ministry and taking on a small minority who viciously attacked Paul's apostolic credentials.							***Date:*** Summer AD 56, in 3rd missionary journey ***Recipients:*** The Gentile church at Corinth ***Origination:*** From Macedonia on his way to Corinth.
INTRODUCTION 1:1–11	**BODY OF THE LETTER 1:12–13:10**							**CONCLUSION 13:11–14**
	ANSWERING CONCERNS ABOUT PAUL'S MINISTRY 1:12–7:16			**APPEAL FOR THE JERUSALEM FUND 8:1–9:15**	**RESPONDING TO ACCUSATIONS BY REBELLIOUS LEADERS 10:1–13:10**			
Greetings of Grace 1:1–2 **Doxology on God's Comfort 1:3–11** Abounding Troubles & Comfort 1:3–5 Sharing Gospel Sorrows & Joys 1:6–7 Delivered from Great Affliction in Asia 1:8–11	**Problems with Paul's Itinerary Discussed 1:12–2:13** Explanation of Paul's Revised Itinerary & Unplanned Absence 1:12–2:4 Instructions for Restoring the Notorious Sinner in Paul's Absence 2:5–11 Report of Paul's Recent Depression over the Corinthians 2:12–13	***INTERLUDE:* The Glory of the Gospel Ministry 2:14–7:4** Divine Commiss-ioning for the Gospel Ministry 2:14–3:18 Endurance in the Ministry Empowered by Glory & Hope 4:1–5:10 The Ministry of Recon-ciliation 5:11–6:10 Closing Appeal for Their Recon-ciliation 6:11–7:4	**Problems with Paul's Itinerary Resolved 7:5–16** Paul's Comfort from Titus's Report 7:5–7 Paul's Joy in their Repentance 7:8–13a Paul's Renewed Confidence in the Corinthians 7:13b–16	Examples of Gracious Giving 8:1–15 The Plan for Gathering the Collection 8:16–9:15	**Paul's Upstanding Apostolic Ministry 10:1–12:13** Paul's Leadership with Humility & Authority 10:1–11:15 Paul's Uncomfor-table Boasting of His Résumé 11:16–12:13	**Paul's Upcoming Apostolic Visit 12:14–13:10** The Relief Fund Not a Money Ploy 12:14–18 The Visit Intended for their Growth 12:19–21 Warning of the Upcoming Confron-tation with the Unrepentant 13:1–10		**Concluding Commands 13:11** **Farewell Greetings 13:12–13** **Closing Prayer 13:14**

CHART 40: Focus on 2 Corinthians 1:12–7:16

INTRODUCTION, 1:1–11

BODY OF THE LETTER, 1:12–13:10

ANSWERING CONCERNS ABOUT PAUL'S MINISTRY, 1:12–7:16

Problems with Paul's Itinerary Discussed 1:12–2:13	INTERLUDE: The Glory of the Gospel Ministry 2:14–7:4				Problems with Paul's Itinerary Resolved 7:5–16
	Divine Commissioning for the Gospel Ministry 2:14–4:6	**Endurance in the Ministry Empowered by Glory & Hope 4:7–5:10**	**The Ministry of Reconciliation 5:11–6:10**	**Closing Appeal for Reconcil-iation 6:11–7:4**	
Explanation of Paul's Revised Itinerary & Unplanned Absence 1:12–2:4	Christ Always Leads the Ministry in Triumph 2:14–16	Unending Endurance 4:7–18	The Focus of the Ministry 5:11–21	A Plea for Their Heart 6:11–13	Paul's Comfort from Titus's Report 7:5–7
Defense of His Integrity & Intentions 1:12–14	The Spirit's Commendation of Paul in the Corinthians 2:17–3:3	*God's Power Within to Endure Ongoing Trials 4:7–12*	*Persuading Men unto Christ 5:11–15*	Their Need to Separate from Some Sinners 6:14–18	Paul's Joy in their Repentance 7:8–13a
Visits Postponed Not in Deceit but for Their Benefit 1:15–24	Called into the Gloriously Superior New Covenant 3:4–18	*Boldness in the Present, Confidence in the Resurrection 4:13–15*	*Spiritual Transformation 5:16–17*	Final Appeal to Reconcile with Paul 7:1–4	Paul's Renewed Confidence in the Corinthians 7:13b–16
His Decision to Write Before Coming Again 2:1–4	*The Greater Glory of the New Covenant thru the Spirit 3:4–11*	*Future Glory to Outweigh All Afflictions 4:16–18*	*Reconciliation with God thru Christ 5:18–21*		
Instructions on Restoring the Notorious Sinner in Paul's Absence 2:5–11	*A Greater Boldness than Moses Before God & Men 3:12–18*	Heavenly Mindedness 5:1–10	The Integrity of the Ministry 6:1–10		
Report of Paul's Recent Depression over the Corinthians 2:12–13	*A Proclamation of the Glory of God in Christ 4:1–6*	*Eager for a Heavenly Home 5:1–8*	*Making Sincere Appeals 6:1–3*		
		Ready to Give Account to Christ 5:9–10	*Serving Faithfully Despite Suffering 6:4–10*		

APPEAL TO GIVE TO THE JERUSALEM FUND, 8:1–9:15

RESPONDING TO ACCUSATIONS BY REBELLIOUS LEADERS, 10:1–13:10

CONCLUSION, 13:11–14

CHART 41: Focus on 2 Corinthians 8:1–13:10

INTRODUCTION, 1:1–11

BODY OF THE LETTER, 1:12–13:10

ANSWERING CONCERNS ABOUT PAUL'S MINISTRY, 1:12–7:16

APPEAL TO GIVE TO THE JERUSALEM FUND 8:1–9:15

Examples of Gracious Giving 8:1–15

- The Example of the Poor Macedonian Churches 8:1–7
  - *Lavish Gifts Despite Poverty 8:1–5*
  - *An Example to Corinth 8:6–7*
- The Example of the Lord Jesus Christ 8:8–9
- The Example of the Corinthians' Earlier Involvement 8:10–15

The Plan for Gathering the Collection 8:16–9:15

- Authorization of Titus & Reputable Brothers 8:16–24
- The Concern Not to Shame the Sacrificial Macedonians 9:1–5
- Encouragement to Give to the Fund 9:6–15
  - *Give Generously & Cheerfully 9:6–7*
  - *Give Trusting in God's Gracious Reward 9:8–11*
  - *Give Knowing that It Multiplies Thanksgiving 9:12–14*
  - *Think of God's Indescribable Gift 9:15*

RESPONDING TO ACCUSATIONS BY REBELLIOUS LEADERS 10:1–13:10

Paul's Upstanding Apostolic Ministry 10:1–12:13

Paul's Leadership with Humility & Authority 10:1–11:15

- His Desire to be Gentle 10:1–2
- His Readiness to Fight 10:3–11
  - *Against Falsehood with Spiritual Warfare 10:3–6*
  - *Against False Teachers in Corinth 10:7–11*
- His Commendation from God 10:12–18
- His Concern over Their Deception 11:1–15
  - *Their Susceptibility to False Teachers 11:1–6*
  - *Their Misunderstanding of His Finances 11:7–11*
  - *Their Following after False Apostles 11:12–15*

Paul's Uncomfortable Boasting of His Résumé 11:16–12:13

- His Regrettable Need for Boasting 11:16–21
- His Jewish Heritage & Sufferings in Ministry 11:22–33
- His Special Revelations 12:1–10
  - *A Glorious Vision of Heaven 12:1–6*
  - *A Humbling Thorn in the Flesh 12:7–10*
- His Apostolic Signs Humbly Employed 12:11–13

Paul's Upcoming Apostolic Visit 12:14–13:10

- The Relief Fund Not a Money Ploy 12:14–18
- The Visit Intended for Their Growth 12:19–21
- The Coming Confrontation with the Unrepentant 13:1–10
  - *The Plan to Confront Unrepentant Leaders & Remove Them 13:1–4*
  - *The Urge for Self-Examination Rather than Apostolic Reproof 13:5–10*

CONCLUSION, 13:11–14

THE EPISTLE TO THE GALATIANS

Paul's letter to Galatians was probably written around AD 49, perhaps his first inspired letter. It was composed shortly before the Jerusalem Council (AD 49) where the issue of the Gentiles' membership in the church was officially settled. In this letter Paul corrects a grave error taking root in Galatia, the idea that Gentile believers must first become circumcised before being recognized as Christians.

This epistle is a circular letter, written to churches in the region of Galatia. Galatia was a Roman province in Asia Minor, the southern portion of which Paul had evangelized during his first missionary journey (AD 46–47, Acts 13–14). Afterwards, false teachers from Jerusalem crept in, teaching Gentile Christians the circumcision heresy. Paul argues forcefully that this teaching fundamentally contradicts the Gospel.

Paul confronts the error head-on in the letter's introduction (1:8–9), pronouncing a curse on any proclaimer of a false gospel. The body of the letter divides into three parts. In the first portion, Paul writes autobiographically, sharing his own experience in the gospel and the ministry (1:10–2:21). Even though he previously confronted Peter in Antioch about giving ground to Judaizers, Paul stresses his unity with the Jerusalem church. The real outsiders were not Paul and company but the false teachers. Paul reminds his readers of the gospel they'd first learned and calls them to live in light of that truth. In the second portion, Paul expounds on the simplicity of the gospel by showing how justification by faith was taught in the OT and exposing the circumcision gospel as a form of spiritual slavery (3:1–4:31). In the final section, he applies gospel truths to the Christian life, stressing how the Spirit makes the Christian fruitful instead of defiled by the works of the flesh (5:1–6:10).

THE EPISTLE TO THE EPHESIANS

Paul's letter to the Ephesians was written during his first Roman imprisonment (c. AD 61). Colossians and Philemon were written around the same time, delivered by Tychicus (6:21–22). This epistle appears to be a circular letter for Asia Minor as is evidenced by the lack of personal greetings in the conclusion and the lack of the phrase "in Ephesus" (1:1) in some very ancient copies of the letter. Ephesus, the leading city of western Asia Minor, no doubt received it first. Paul instructs Gentile Christians about their place in God's plan and calls them to live in light of their holy and enriching calling.

The introduction includes a rich doxology thanking the triune God for His redeeming grace. The body of the epistle divides in two. The first half is loaded with doctrinal instruction about God's calling the Gentiles into the Church (1:15–3:21). Paul opens and closes this half with instructive prayers in which he recounts how Christ's riches and God's grace were bestowed on Gentile believers. In between these prayers he stresses how their salvation from darkness came only by grace through faith, not by works of the Law. They were now united with believing Jews in one universal Church. Paul explains how he was specially (and not without controversy) called to take the gospel to Gentiles who now have equal place in the Church along with believing Jews.

In the second half, Paul discusses practical considerations of living in light of God's grace (4:1–6:20). They must labor to preserve the unity of the Church in the Spirit, recognizing their diversities but emphasizing their common purpose in Christ. Intent on one purpose, they will live differently than the world, walk in God's love and light, and wage successful spiritual warfare while outfitted with God's armor. The letter concludes with a prayer for God's blessing on the Gentile readers.

CHART 42 Galatians ©2015 M. Scott Bashoor	***Purpose:*** Paul warns the Galatians not to tolerate any addition to the gospel of grace, particularly ritual circumcision, because a Gentile following Jesus does not need first to become a Jew.	***Date:*** Perhaps AD 49, before the Jerusalem Council ***Recipients:*** The Gentile churches in Galatia ***Origination:*** Paul's whereabouts unknown

	BODY OF THE LETTER 1:11–6:10			
INTRODUCTION 1:1–9	**DEFENSE OF PAUL'S APOSTLESHIP: AUTOBIOGRAPHY OF HIS GOSPEL MINISTRY 1:10–2:21**	**DIRECT APPEAL TO THE GALATIANS: EXPLANATION OF THE GOSPEL'S SIMPLICITY 3:1–4:31**	**LIVING THE GOSPEL IN GALATIA: APPLICATION OF THE GOSPEL'S CERTAINTIES 5:1–6:10**	**CONCLUSION 6:11–18**
Greetings of Grace 1:1–5 Paul's Divine Appointment 1:1 Salutation 1:2 Greetings & Doxology 1:3–5 **Initial Charge 1:6–9** Amazement at their Capitulation 1:6–7 Threat of Divine Curse 1:8–9	**Paul's Experience of the Gospel 1:10–17** God's Calling & Approval, Not Man's 1:10–12 His Former Life, Conversion & Earliest Ministry 1:13–17 **Paul's Fellowship with Jerusalem 1:18–2:10** First Visit & Fourteen-Year Ministry in the North 1:18–24 Second Visit: Confronting the Circumcision Heresy, Receiving Affirmation 2:1–10 **Paul Correction of Peter at Antioch 2:11–21** Rebuke for Refusing Gentile Table Fellowship 2:11–14 Justification by Faith as the Basis of Fellowship 2:15–21	**The Galatians' Experience of the Gospel 3:1–5** **Justification by Faith in the Old Testament 3:6–14** **The Limited Scope of the Mosaic Law 3:15–25** The Abrahamic Covenant Precedes It 3:15–19 The Law's Role as Tutor, Not Savior 3:20–25 **Gospel Transformation into Sons 3:26–4:7** Both Jews & Gentiles are Sons by Faith 3:26–29 No Longer Slaves but Sons 4:1–7 **The Slavery of a False Gospel 4:8–31** Fear that They Not Return to Slavery 4:8–11 An Appeal Recalling Their Former Loyalty 4:12–20 The Allegory of Hagar & Sarah 4:21–31	**A Warning of Falling from Grace 5:1–12** Charge to Stand Firm in Christ's Freedom 5:1 Faith in Circumcision Nullifies Grace 5:2–6 Choose Circumcision or the Cross 5:7–12 **The New Life of Love & Righteousness 5:13–26** Freed by Christ to Love 5:13–15 Walking in the Spirit Not the Flesh 5:16–21 The Fruit of the Spirit 5:22–26 **Bearing Burdens & Meeting Needs 6:1–10** Bear One Another's Burdens 6:1–3 Bear One's Own Burdens 6:4–5 Sharing & Sowing into One Another's Lives 6:6–10	**Validating Signature 6:11** **Final Salvo 6:12–15** Circumcision Doctrine, a Sham Gospel 6:12–13 Christ, the Only Boast 6:14–15 **Farewell 6:16–18** Peace on the Faithful 6:16–17 Closing Prayer 6:18

CHART 43 Ephesians ©2015 M. Scott Bashoor	***Purpose:*** Paul teaches Gentile Christians about their place in God's plan for the Church and about their responsibility to live appropriately in light of that holy and enriching calling.	***Date:*** *c.* AD 61 ***Recipients:*** Ephesus and other regional Gentile churches ***Origination:*** During Paul's 1st Roman imprisonment

INTRODUCTION 1:1–14	**BODY OF THE LETTER 1:15–6:20**								**CONCLUSION 6:21–24**
	DOCTRINAL CONSIDERATIONS: GOD'S CALLING OF GENTILES INTO THE CHURCH BY HIS GRACE 1:15–3:21				**PRACTICAL IMPLICATIONS: PAUL'S COUNSEL ON LIVING LIFE IN LIGHT OF GOD'S GRACE 4:1–6:20**				
Greetings of Grace 1:1–2 **Doxology on Saving Grace 1:3–14** Chosen by the Father 1:3–6 Redeemed by the Son 1:7–12 *Enriched by Grace 1:7–8a* *Culminating in Glory 1:8b–12* Sealed by the Spirit 1:13–14	**Instructive Opening Prayer for Them 1:15–23** Thanksgiving for Their Faith & Love 1:15–16 Prayer for Growth in Divine Enlightenment 1:17–23 *In the Riches of Christ 1:17–19a* *In the Surpassing Power & Authority of Christ 1:19b–23*	**Salvation by Grace thru Faith 2:1–10** Their Prior Lost Estate 2:1–3 God's Mercy & Grace Revealed in Christ 2:4–10 *God's Mercies to Sinners 2:4–7* *Salvation by Grace, Not by Works 2:8–10*	**Unity of Jew & Gentile in the Church 2:11– 3:13** Unity in Christ 2:11–22 *Gentiles Once Excluded, Now Included 2:11–13* *The One New Man 2:14–18* *God's New Household 2:19–22* The Mystery of the Gentiles' Inclusion Revealed by Paul 3:1–13 *Paul's Unique Ministry 3:1–3* *A New Revelation 3:4–7* *Paul's Ministry of Glorious Truth to the World 3:8–13*	**Closing Prayer of Petition 3:14–21** Empowerment thru Understanding God's Rich Grace 3:14–19 Doxology on Christ's Glory in the Church 3:20–21	**Preserve the Church's Unity in the Spirit 4:1–16** Oneness of the Diverse Peoples in the Body 4:1–10 *Plea for Unity 4:1–3* *Singular Commonalities 4:4–6* *The Diversity of Gifts 4:7–11* Uniting Purpose of Diverse Gifts 4:12–16 *Maturity & Unity 4:12–13* *Stability & Body Strength 4:14–16*	**Live Differently than the World 4:17–32** Discard Past Practices 4:17–19 Old Man & New Man 4:20–24 New Ways of Relating to Others & Pleasing God 4:25–32	**Walk in Love, Light & Wisdom 5:1–6:9** Christian Love & Moral Light 5:1–14 *Walk in Love 5:1–2* *Walk in Purity 5:3–6* *Walk in Light 5:7–14* Spiritual Wisdom 5:15–6:9 *Wisdom in General 5:15–17* *Wisdom for Relationships: Spouses, Children, Slaves 5:18–6:9*	**Engage in Spiritual Warfare 6:10–20** Gospel Armor for Believers' Spiritual Defense 6:10–17 *The Nature of the Battle 6:10–12* *The Taking Up of Arms 6:13–17* Needed Prayers for the Gospel's Advance 6:18–20	**Validation of the Courier, Tychicus 6:21–22** **Final Prayer of Blessing 6:23–24**

THE EPISTLE TO THE PHILIPPIANS

Paul's letter to Philippians was written during his first Roman imprisonment (c. AD 62). Written a year after Ephesians and Colossians, it is placed between them in modern Bibles because of its length **(see chart 69)**. This warm letter gives thanks for their sacrificial support and addresses a rift between two key workers. Paul encourages the church to maintain a joyful unity in the gospel lest their work for the Lord be hindered by conflicts and divisive influences.

The Philippian church was the first Paul founded after receiving the Macedonian call in his second missionary journey (AD 49–51, Acts 15:40–18:22). Paul had a uniquely trusting relationship with them, making an exception in receiving their financial gifts. During his imprisonment they sent a generous gift, and the courier informed him of conflicts which Paul lovingly addresses. After greeting them, offering thanks for their gifts, and praying for their love (1:1–11), he updates them on the gospel's progress in Rome despite his imprisonment, a predicament he's confident will soon end (1:12–26). In the second section Paul exhorts them to strive together joyfully in gospel service (1:27–2:30). This requires humility of mind as most perfectly seen in Christ's incarnation and as emulated by gospel workers they knew. The third section warns them of false teachers who were looking for footholds in churches (3:1–4:1). Any doctrine contrary to the that of Christ and Scripture must be rejected. In the fourth section, Paul specifically addresses the rift between two key Christian women, encouraging all to pursue peace and joy in the Lord through prayer and right thinking (4:2–9). In the conclusion, Paul again thanks them for their gifts and assures them of God's care for him and them (4:10–23).

THE EPISTLE TO THE COLOSSIANS

Paul's letter to the Colossians was written during his first Roman imprisonment (c. AD 61) at the same time as Ephesians and Philemon. There is much similar content and wording in Colossians and Ephesians, but the problems in Colossae were somewhat unique. While Paul had never visited this church, he had special care for it because it was founded by members of his missionary team. He'd heard the church was troubled by a unique form of false teaching blending the Judaizers' errors with indigenous philosophies. The epistle teaches Christians about the preeminence of Christ over all things, and how their union with Him should lead them away from false teaching and into righteous conduct for His glory.

After opening the letter with greetings and a prayer for their fruitfulness in the transforming knowledge of Christ (1:1–14), Paul expounds on Christ's preeminence and His gospel ministry to the Gentiles (1:15–29). Christ is head over everything, including the work of reconciliation the Colossians had experienced with God. This was in line with the mission to the Gentiles to which Paul was uniquely entrusted. In the letter's second section, he confronts the false teachings threatening their understanding of Christ's supremacy (2:1–23). Such heresies were incompatible with their union with the divine Christ. These errors of ritual observances and fanciful philosophies were powerless inventions of the world, not the revelation of God in Christ. In the final section (3:1–4:6), Paul applies the truth of union with Christ to practical affairs of life. Union with Christ requires centering one's mind on heavenly things, reckoning inner renewal to be true, and then relating to others with a renewed mind. In the conclusion, the apostle affirms the courier, Tychicus, as his representative before passing on personal greetings and instructions related to the gospel work (4:7–18).

CHART 44 Philippians ©2015 M. Scott Bashoor	***Purpose:*** Paul encourages the Philippians to work hard at maintaining a joyful unity in their common life of the gospel so their work for the Lord might not be hindered by relational conflicts or threatened by false teachers who might polarize them.	***Date:*** *c.* AD 62 ***Recipients:*** The Gentile church at Philippi ***Origination:*** Paul's 1st Roman imprisonment

INTRODUCTION 1:1–11	**BODY OF THE LETTER 1:12–4:9**				**CONCLUSION 4:10–23**
Greetings of Grace 1:1–2 **Paul's Prayers for Them 1:3–11** Ongoing Thanksgiving for Their Ongoing Partnership 1:3–8 Prayers for Their Abounding Love 1:9–11	**ENCOURAGING REPORT ABOUT PAUL'S CASE AND MINISTRY 1:12–26**	**EXHORTATION TO JOYFULLY STRIVE TOGETHER WITH CHRIST-LIKE HUMILITY 1:27–2:30**	**CONCERNS ABOUT FALSE TEACHERS' THREAT TO THEIR UNIFIED PURSUIT OF CHRIST 3:1–4:1**	**CONCLUDING APPLICATIONS ON MAINTAINING UNITY 4:2–9**	**Paul's Contented Receipt for Their Sacrificial Gift 4:10–20** Expression of Thanks and Example of Contentment 4:10–14 Recount of their Giving History & Assurance of God's Supply 4:15–20 **Final Exchange of Greetings 4:21–22** **Closing Prayer 4:23**
	The Advance of the Gospel Despite Paul's Imprisonment 1:12–18a *Paul's Story & Message Spread Thru Rome 1:12–13* *Conflicting Opinions on Paul in the Church Notwithstanding 1:14–18a* Paul's Confidence in His Situation 1:18b–26 *A Positive Legal Outcome Expected 1:18b–20* *Longing for His Eternal Home but Zealous to Continue Service Below 1:21–26*	Live Worthy of Their Heavenly Citizenship 1:27–30 Fulfill One Another's Joy by Jointly Practicing Humility 2:1–4 Follow the Example of Christ's Humility 2:5–11 Be United as a Living Light in a Dark World 2:12–16 Imitate Men with the Mind of Christ 2:17–30 *Paul 2:17–18* *Timothy 2:19–24* *Epaphroditus 2:25–30*	Joy in the Lord to Withstand Error 3:1 The Dangerous and Growing Problem of the False Workers (e.g., Judaizers) 3:2–3 The Single-minded Pursuit of Nothing Other than the Knowledge of Christ 3:4–16 *Past Religious Accomplishments Worthless 3:4–7* *The Surpassing Value of Christ's Righteousness & Resurrection Power 3:8–11* *Paul's Resolve to Pursue Christ & Exhortation for All to Follow Together 3:12–16* A Warning against False Ministers 3:17–4:1 *Beware the Enemies of the Cross 3:17–19* *Maintain Heavenly Identity & Confidence 3:20–4:1*	Mediated Peacemaking Needed between Christian Workers 4:2–3 The Church's Pursuit of Personal & Relational Peace 4:4–9 *Joy in the Lord 4:4* *Gentleness 4:5* *Prayer & Peace 4:6–7* *Right Thinking 4:8* *Godly Imitation 4:9*	

CHART 45 Colossians ©2014 M. Scott Bashoor	***Purpose:*** Paul teaches Gentile Christians about the preeminence of Christ over all things, and how their union with him should lead them away from false teaching and into righteous conduct to His glory.	***Date:*** *c.* AD 61 ***Recipients:*** The Gentile church at Colossae ***Origination:*** During Paul's 1st Roman imprisonment

INTRODUCTION 1:1–14	BODY OF THE LETTER 1:14–4:6			CONCLUSION 4:7–18
	CHRIST'S PREEMINENCE & THE GOSPEL MINISTRY 1:15–29	FALSE TEACHINGS IN COLOSSAE THREATENING SUPREMACY OVER THE THINGS OF CHRIST 2:1–2:23	PRACTICAL IMPLICATIONS OF LIVING LIFE IN UNION WITH CHRIST 3:1–4:6	
Greetings of Grace 1:1–2 **Paul's Prayers for Them 1:3–14** Thanksgiving for their Fruitfulness 1:3–8 Prayers for Growth in the Transforming Know-ledge of Christ 1:9–14	**Christ's Preeminence over Everything 1:15–20** Lord of Creation 1:15–17 Lord of Redemption 1:18–20 **God's Reconciliation of the Colossians thru Christ 1:21–23** **Paul's Ministry of Hope to the Gentiles thru Christ 1:24–29** Paul's Hope in Suffering 1:24 Paul's Stewardship of the Mystery of the Gospel to Gentiles 1:25–27 Paul's Labor of Love to Present Gentiles Complete in Christ 1:28–29	**Concern for their Continuation in Truth 2:1–8** Efforts from a Distance to Promote the Truth 2:1–5 Charge to Resist False Philosophies 2:6–8 **The Incomparability of Union with Christ 2:9–15** Christ is the Very Fullness of Deity 2:9 Union with Christ brings Spiritual Completion, Spiritual Circumcision & Cancelation of Sin 2:10–14 Christ is the Conqueror of all Devils 2:15 **Confrontation of False Teachings 2:16–23** Calendar Keeping, Asceticism & False Supernaturalism Fall Short of Christ 2:16–19 False Philosophies are Powerless Inventions of the World 2:20–23	**Center Your Mind on Heavenly Things 3:1–4** **Reckon Your Christian Renewal to be True 3:5–11** Consider Your Old Self Dead 3:5–9 Consider Yourself Renewed 3:10–11 **Relate to Others with a Renewed Mind 3:12–4:6** Relationships within the Church 3:12–17 Relationships in Christian Households: Spouses, Children, Slaves 3:18–4:1 Relationships in the World 4:2–6	**Endorsement of Tychichus & Onesimus 4:7–9** **Personal Greetings from Friends in Rome 4:10–14** **Greetings & Instructions for those in Laodicea 4:15–17** **Paul's Personal Sign-Off 4:18**

THE EPISTLES TO THE THESSALONIANS

Paul's two letters to the Thessalonians were written in AD 51 and 52 respectively. Paul founded their church during his second missionary journey (AD 49–51) but he had to leave abruptly due to a violent reaction from unbelieving Jews (Acts 17:5–10). In Corinth months later, he learned of troubles in this largely Gentile church that required attention, and this began a series of exchanges including these two letters.

Paul writes **First Thessalonians** to assure the church of his love despite his absence, and to assure them of Jesus' love who had called them to live holy lives in light of His Second Coming. There were doubts in their minds about Paul's care for them since he had been absent so long, and false ideas about Christian living and the Second Coming were percolating. Paul begins by greeting them and thanking God for their faithful testimony (1 Thess 1:1–10). The first half of the epistle begins with Paul assuring them of their relationship and explaining his team's absence (1 Thess 2:1–3:13). He reminds them of the genuineness of the team's ministry and reveals how they've been continually thankful for their reception of the gospel and ongoing witness. He explains why they departed suddenly and were not able to return. Though only Timothy would be going back to them, Paul assures the young church of the whole team's love and gratitude. In the second half, Paul makes practical exhortations in light of the Lord's Second Coming (1 Thess 4:1–5:22). The Christian life requires living for God's pleasure and the benefit of others, not sinful pleasures and selfishness. There was some confusion about the estate of those who died before the Lord's return, so Paul assured them of their participation in the future resurrection. The knowledge of the Lord's coming leads to a life of spiritual sobriety, and such godliness is best pursued under spiritual authority in a community of peace and love. The letter concludes (1 Thess 5:23–28) with prayers, instructions, and blessings.

Second Thessalonians, written some months later, acknowledges that most had responded well to the first letter but that some problems had grown worse. An element in the church was teaching that the Second Coming had already occurred, leading some to think they were in a new era in which the earlier instruction on Christian living no longer applied. Paul urged the church to discipline out of their midst those who accepted this false teaching and then remained unrepentant. Meanwhile, he urges the church to actively support the ministry of the gospel. Paul encourages the Thessalonians' steadfastness in their faith, comforting them amidst persecutions, and correcting false notions of the Second Coming that troubled them and led some into idleness.

In the introduction, Paul joyfully acknowledges that a wave of persecution had not stopped the church, assures them of their future vindication, and prays for more gospel progress (1:1–12). In the first half of the letter, he corrects the false notion circulating that the Day of the Lord had already occurred (2 Thess 2:1–17). He explains that the great falling away and the arrival of the Anti-Christ are yet to come. He encourages them about the church's place in God's plan as chosen ones for His glory. In the second half, he exhorts them to prayer and practical obedience, giving instructions on how to deal with an element of idle troublemakers that must be disciplined out of the church for the good of the whole (2 Thess 3:1–15). Paul concludes the letter by praying for God's peace and blessing upon them (2 Thess 3:16–18).

CHART 46 **1 Thessalonians** ©2015 M. Scott Bashoor	***Purpose:*** Paul encourages the Thessalonians that despite his absence they are truly loved by him and even more so by Christ, who has called them to pursue holiness and embrace hope in light of his Second Coming.	***Date:*** *c.* AD 51, during Paul's 2nd missionary journey ***Recipients:*** The Gentile church at Thessalonica ***Origination:*** During Paul's extended stay in Corinth

INTRODUCTION 1:1–10	**BODY OF THE LETTER 2:1–5:22**						**CONCLUSION 5:23–28**
	ENCOURAGEMENTS ABOUT THEIR RELATIONSHIP & EXPLANATIONS FOR THE APOSTOLIC TEAM'S ABSENCE 2:1–3:13			**PRACTICAL EXHORTATIONS FOR THE BELIEVERS & THE CHURCH IN LIGHT OF THE LORD'S SECOND COMING 4:1–5:22**			
Greetings of Grace 1:1 **Paul's Thanksgiving for Them 1:2–10** Thankful for Their Constancy in God's Calling 1:2–5 Thankful for Their Extensive Testimony 1:6–10	**Reminder of the Team's Genuine Ministry in Thessa-lonica 2:1–12** Not Done in Vain 2:1 Not Done for Gain or Glory 2:2–6 Was Done in Selfless Love 2:7–12	**Declaration of Team's Continuing Thankful-ness 2:13–16** For the Church's Initial Reception of the Gospel 2:13 For the Church's Courageous Witness 2:14–16	**Explanation of the Team's Departure & Continued Absence 2:17–3:13** Paul's Frustrated Desire to Return to Them 2:17–20 Decision to Send Timothy Instead 3:1–8 The Team's Ongoing Thanksgiving & Intercession for Them 3:9–13	**Living the Christian Life for God's Holy Pleasure 4:1–12** A Reminder of Earlier Teaching 4:1–2 The Imperative of Sexual Purity 4:3–8 The Balance of Mutual Care & Personal Employment 4:9–12	**Living in Confident Hope in God's Final Plans 4:13–5:11** Hope for Those Who Die Before the Lord's Return 4:13–18 Instructions for Living in Light of the Day of the Lord 5:1–11 *The Suddenness of the Lord's Coming 5:1–3* *Sobriety of Life in the Present 5:4–8* *The Promise of Final Salvation in Christ 5:9–11*	**Living in Christian Community According to Christ's Will 5:12–22** Honoring Those in Spiritual Authority 5:12–13a Pursuing Mutual Peace & Care 5:13b–15 Practicing the Piety of Prayerfulness 5:16–18 Affirming God's Revelation 5:19–21 Avoiding All Manifest-ations of Evil 5:22	**Confident Prayer of Blessing 5:23–24** **Prayer Requested for the Team 5:25** **Appeal to Greet One Another 5:26** **Command for the Public Reading of the Letter 5:27** **Final Prayer of Blessing 5:28**

CHART 47 **2 Thessalonians** ©2015 M. Scott Bashoor	***Purpose:*** Paul encourages the Thessalonians' steadfastness in their faith, comforting them amidst persecutions and correcting false notions of the Second Coming that troubled them and led some into idleness.	***Date:*** *c.* AD 52, during Paul's 2nd missionary journey ***Recipients:*** The Gentile church at Thessalonica ***Origination:*** During Paul's extended stay in Corinth

INTRODUCTION **1:1–12**	**BODY OF THE LETTER** **2:1–3:15**				**CONCLUSION** **3:16–18**
	ENCOURAGING CORRECTION: **THE CHURCH TO ESCAPE THE DAY OF THE LORD** **2:1–17**		**CHALLENGING EXHORTATIONS:** **THE NEED FOR PRAYER & PRACTICAL OBEDIENCE** **3:1–15**		
Greetings of Grace **1:1–2** **Prayers from the Apostolic Team for Them** **1:3–12** Thankful for Their Growth in the Faith Amidst Persecution 1:3–4 Confident in God's Final Vindication 1:5–10 Prayerful for the Continued Progress of God's Glory in Them 1:11–12	**False Teachings about the Day of the Lord** **2:1–12** Circulation of False Teachings 2:1–2 Correction of Misconceptions 2:3–12 *The Great Apostasy & Anti-Christ Is Yet to Come* *2:3–4* *End-of-the-Age Evil is Present but Restrained* *2:5–7* *The Great Deception Will Empty into Judgment* *2:8–12*	**Encouragement about the Church's Place in God's Plan** **2:13–17** The Thessalonians Chosen for God's Glory 2:13–14 The Thessalonians Exhorted to Continued Faithfulness 2:15 The Thessalonians Encouraged thru the Team's Prayer 2:16–17	**The Need for Prayer** **3:1–5** Prayer Requested for the Apostolic Team 3:1–2 Confidence Expressed in God's Faithfulness 3:3–4 Prayer Offered for the Thessalonians 3:5	**The Need for Practical Obedience** **3:6–15** Discipline Required for the Unruly 3:6 The Apostolic Team's Example & Instruction Regarding Work & Self-Reliance 3:7–10 Challenge to Idle Troublemakers 3:11–12 Encouragement for the Faithful 3:13 Instructions on Implementing Discipline 3:14–15	**Prayer for God's Peace & Presence** **3:16** **Personal Authentication of the Letter** **3:17** **Final Prayer of Blessing** **3:18**

THE PASTORAL EPISTLES

The last collection of Paul's writings contains epistles addressed to individual church leaders after whom each letter is named. Technically, only Philemon was a pastor. Timothy and Titus were apostolic delegates in Ephesus and on Crete, so their authority was more enhanced than Philemon's.

First Timothy is Paul's authorization to execute reforms in the Ephesian church by confronting an intrusion of false teaching breeding confusion and disorder to the church. After Paul's release from prison (c. AD 63), he circled back through the churches in the East where, true to his earlier prophecy (Acts 20:29), he discovered significant errors at Ephesus. This letter was sent after leaving Timothy there in AD 65 to sort out problems. The body of the letter opens with a charge to confront the false teaching (1:3–20). Order needed to be restored in the church, including the proper roles of men and women in worship and the appointment of qualified overseers and deacons (2:1–3:13). Paul's goal before his next visit was to see the church promote proper conduct, center itself on Christ, and resist the tide of false teaching (3:13–4:5). After personally encouraging Timothy in his spiritual life and faithful service (4:6–16), he gives instructions for different groups in the church including widows, elders, and slaves (5:1-6:2). The letter closes with Paul's final charge to counter the false teachers and to live a life of godly contentment (6:3–19).

Second Timothy is Paul's final letter, written c. AD 68. Paul is imprisoned again in Rome and expects martyrdom. He gives final instructions for Timothy's reforms in Ephesus before returning to him. After an introduction of greetings and thankful prayer (1:1 5), the letter's first half is a challenge to preserve in gospel ministry despite mounting persecution (1:6–2:13). Here, he calls Timothy to boldness and endurance in the face of persecution and hardship. In the second half, Paul charges him to preserve gospel fidelity despite growing apostasy (2:14–4:8). He charges him to counter the surge of false teaching in the church and warns it will worsen. In a final charge Timothy is placed under divine obligation to preach the word at all costs. The letter concludes urging Timothy to come to Rome as soon as possible to Paul's aid (4:9–22).

Titus (c. AD 65) is Paul's authorization to execute reforms in the churches on the island of Crete. Paul stationed Titus there to reestablish order in the churches by appointing godly leaders, confronting false teaching, and teaching gospel-motivated conduct in a place notorious for licentious living. After an introduction that publicly validates Titus (1:1–4), the body of the letters begins with a formal charge to appoint godly leaders equipped to counter the false teachers (1:5–16). Paul writes next about what gospel-shaped conduct looks like in relationships between various ages, genders, and stations of life (2:1–15). Finally, Paul teaches about how believers ought to engage with the outside world (3:1–11) by obeying governing authorities, understanding the world's need for redemption, and turning unrepentant schismatics back to the world.

Philemon was written by Paul at the same time as Ephesians and Colossians (c. AD 61) to an elder at the church in Colossae. He urges Philemon to accept as a ministry partner his returning runaway slave, Onesimus, who had been converted and discipled by Paul. Paul opens with words of greetings and prayers of thanks (vv. 1–7) before appealing to his friend to forgive Onesimus and publicly receive him as a ministry partner (vv. 8–20). Paul's appeal is based on his friendship with Philemon and their common experience of grace. He concludes with affirmations of Philemon's character and his expectation to visit soon.

CHART 48 **1 Timothy** ©2015 M. Scott Bashoor	***Purpose:*** Paul writes to Timothy, whom he recently stationed at Ephesus, to confront an intrusion of false teaching that had brought confusion and disorder to the church. Timothy must guard the truth and reform the church.	***Date:*** *c.* AD 65 ***Recipient:*** Timothy, Paul's legate in Ephesus ***Origination:*** Paul is ministering in Macedonia after his 1st Roman imprisonment

INTRODUCTION **1:1–2**	**BODY OF THE LETTER:** **Contending for the Truth, Caring for the Church** **1:3–6:19**							**CONCLUSION** **6:20–21**
	OPENING CHARGE: CONFRONT & CORRECT THE FALSE TEACHING **1:3–20**	**ESTABLISHING ORDER IN THE CHURCH** **2:1–3:13**	**PURPOSE OF THE LETTER** **3:14–4:5**	**PERSONAL ADMONITIONS TO TIMOTHY** **4:6–16**	**INSTRUCTIONS REGARDING VARIOUS GROUPS IN THE CHURCH** **5:1–6:2**	**FINAL CHARGE: CONFRONT FALSE TEACHING & GREED** **6:3–19**	
Paul's Apostolic Authority **1:1** **Timothy's Apostolic Validation** **1:2a** **Paul's Greetings of Grace** **1:2b**	**Validation of Timothy as Paul's Envoy** **1:3a** **Correction of the False Teaching in Ephesus** **1:3b–17** The Misuse of the Old Testament & the Law 1:3b–7 The Lawful Use of the Law with the Gospel 1:8–11 Paul's Testimony as a Law Breaker Turned Gospel Minister 1:12–17 **Formal Charge to Confront False Teaching & Teachers** **1:18–20**	**Regarding Public Worship** **2:1–15** Public Prayers for All Men 2:1–7 Men's Leadership 2:8 Women's Participation 2:9–15 **Regarding Church Officers** **3:1–13** Qualifi-cations for Overseers 3:1–7 Qualifi-cations for Deacons 3:8–13	**Preparation for Paul's Visit** **3:14** **Promotion of Proper Church Conduct** **3:15** **Reinforce-ment of the Common Christian Confession** **3:16** **Prophecy about the Rise of False Teachers** **4:1–5**	**Spiritual Discipline Before God** **4:6–10** Nourished on Truth 4:6–7a Disciplined in Spirit 4:7b–9 Laboring in Hope 4:10 **Faithfulness before the Church** **4:11–16** Faithful Teaching & Exemplary Conduct 4:11–13 Perseverance in Personal Devotion 4:15–16	**Relating to Different Ages & Genders** **5:1–2** **Responsibil-ities Toward Widows** **5:3–16** Responsibility of Families 5:3–8 Church Widow Care & Counsel for Widows 5:9–16 **Administrating Elders** **5:17–25** Appropriate Honor & Discipline of Elders 5:17–21 Careful Selection of Elders 5:22–25 **Instructions for Slaves** **6:1–2**	**The Depraved Motives of the False Teachers** **6:3–5** **Correct Thinking on Contentment & True Godliness** **6:6–10** **Formal Charge Regarding Godly Living & Gospel Ministry** **6:11–16** **Instructions on Ministering to Wealthy Believers** **6:17–19**	**Final Charge to Timothy to Guard His Ministry** **6:20–21a** Avoid the Derailments of False Teaching 6:20 Beware of the Seduction of False Teaching 6:21a **Concluding Blessing on the Church** **6:21b**

CHART 49 **2 Timothy** ©2015 M. Scott Bashoor	***Purpose***: Paul writes to Timothy to continue in faithful ministry in Ephesus and beyond despite growing persecution and error, and to come to Paul's assistance in Rome before his execution.	***Date:*** c. AD 67–68 ***Recipient:*** Timothy, Paul's legate in Ephesus ***Origination:*** Paul is again imprisoned in Rome, awaiting final sentencing and execution

INTRODUCTION 1:1–5	BODY OF THE LETTER 1:6–4:8					CONCLUSION 4:9–22
	A CHALLENGE TO PERSEVERE IN GOSPEL MINISTRY DESPITE MOUNTING PERSECUTION 1:6–2:13		A CHARGE TO PRESERVE GOSPEL FIDELITY DESPITE MOUNTING APOSTASY 2:14–4:8			
Greetings of Grace **1:1–2** **Prayer of Thanksgiving** **1:3–5** For Timothy's Fellowship in Ministry 1:3–4 For Timothy's History & Heritage of Faith 1:5	**Boldness in the Face of Persecution** **1:6–18**	**Endurance in the Midst of Hardship** **2:1–13**	**Command to Refute False Teachings** **2:14–26**	**Prophecy of Growing Heresy & Persecution** **3:1–17**	**Paul's Final Words to Timothy** **4:1–8**	**Instructions for Ministry Travel & Transitions** **4:9–15** Paul's Personal Need of Timothy 4:9 Whereabouts of Other Ministry Partners 4:10–12 Special Instructions and Cautions 4:13–15 **Confidence in the Lord's Providence & Deliverance** **4:16–18** **Farewells & Final Instructions** **4:19–22**
	The Command to Kindle Afresh His Service for Christ **1:6–8a** **The Call to Suffer Well in Light of the Gospel's Power** **1:8b–12** **Continue in Gospel Faithfulness** **1:13–18** Paul's Insistence on Timothy's Faithfulness 1:13–14 The Sad Desertion of the Asian Churches 1:15 The Encouragement of Onesiphorus' Ministry 1:16–18	**The Call to be Strong in Christ's Grace** **2:1** **Moving Forward in the Development of Leaders** **2:2** **Illustrations & Examples of Endurance** **2:3–10** The Roman Soldier 2:3–4 The Ancient Athlete 2:5 The Diligent Farmer 2:6 (Prayerful Application Encouraged 2:7) Jesus Christ 2:8 Paul the Prisoner 2:9–10 **A Poem of Confidence in God's Reward for Faithfulness** **2:11–13**	**Avoiding Falsehood & Handling the Truth** **2:14–19** Avoiding Arguments that Distract from Truth 2:14 The Need to Accurately Handle God's Word 2:15 The Corrosive Influence of False Teaching 2:16–19 **Sorting Out Deception in the Lord's House** **2:20–26** Separation from False Teachers & Carnality 2:20–23 Ministry to the Deceived 2:24–26	**The Growing Moral Decay & Defection** **3:1–9** The Advanced Depravity of the False Teachers 3:1–5 The Overthrow of Whole Households by Errorists 3:6–7 The Ancient Illustration of Jannes & Jambres 3:8–9 **The Need for Resolve & Biblical Fidelity** **3:10–17** Paul's Example of Faithfulness & Suffering 3:10–11 The Certainty of Persecution & Apostasy 3:12–13 Timothy's Heritage in Biblical Truth 3:14–17	**Timothy Under Divine Oath & Obligation** **4:1** **The Charge to Preach the Word** **4:2–5** The Formal Charge 2:2 Opposition Expected 2:3–4 Appeal for Timothy's Faithfulness 2:5 **Paul's Encouraging Testimony of Faithful Ministry** **4:6–8** Certain of His End 4:6 Confident of His Reward 4:7–8	

CHART 50 **Titus** ©2015 M. Scott Bashoor	***Purpose***: Paul writes to Titus, recently stationed on Crete, to reestablish order in the churches by appointing godly leaders, confronting false teachers and teaching gospel-motivated conduct. Titus must defend the Gospel and reform the churches.	***Date:*** *c.* AD 65 ***Recipient:*** Titus, Paul's legate on Crete ***Origination:*** Paul ministering in Macedonia after his 1st Roman imprisonment

INTRODUCTION **1:1–4**	**BODY OF THE LETTER** **1:5–3:11**			**CONCLUSION** **3:12–15**
	PAUL'S FORMAL CHARGE TO TITUS: APPOINT GODLY LEADERS WHO CAN COUNTER THE FALSE TEACHERS **1:5–16**	**PAUL'S INSTRUCTIONS FOR GOSPEL-FORMED CONDUCT & RELATIONSHIPS IN THE CHURCHES** **2:1–15**	**PAUL'S INSTRUCTIONS FOR GOSPEL-FORMED RELATIONSHIPS WITH THE OUTSIDE WORLD** **3:1–11**	
Paul's Apostolic Salutation **1:1a** **Paul's Gospel Mission to the Gentiles** **1:1b–3** **Validation of Titus** **1:4a** **Greetings of Grace** **1:4b**	**The Purpose of Titus's Mission: Restore Church Order by Appointing Godly Elders** **1:5** **The Qualifications of Godly Elders** **1:6–9** Personal and Social Character 1:6–8 Doctrinal Clarity and Conviction 1:9 **The Infiltration of False Teachers** **1:10–16** Their Prevalence and Damage 1:10–13a The Mandate to Silence Them 1:13b–14 Their Defilement and Deception 1:15–16	**Standards of Christian Conduct for Various Groups** **2:1–10** The Harmonious Conduct of Different Age Groups and Genders 2:1–8 The Conduct of Slaves before Their Masters 2:9–10 **The Transformative Impact of God's Grace on Conduct & Relationships** **2:11–14** Saving Grace Informs the Soul in Godly Living 2:11–12 Saving Grace Transforms the Soul with Power-Filled Hope 2:13–14 **The Charge for Insistent Teaching on Gospel-Formed Conduct** **2:15**	**Godly Interaction with Ungodly Authorities and All Men** **3:1–2** **A Gospeled Understanding of Human Sinfulness, Christ's Salvation & Christian Conduct** **3:3–8** The Christian's Experience of Sin in His Former Depravity 3:3 The Christian's Experience of Salvation through Christ's Transforming Grace 3:4–7 The Christian's Expression of Faith through Godly Living 3:8 **The Charge to Exclude Unrepentant Schismatics** **3:9–11**	**Instructions Regarding Transitions and Travel** **3:12–14** Titus to Prepare to Transition Out 3:12 Hospitality & Support for Traveling Ministers 3:13–14 **Concluding Greetings to Titus & the Churches** **3:15**

CHART 51 Philemon ©2015 M. Scott Bashoor	***Purpose*:** Paul urges Philemon to accept as a ministry partner his returning runaway slave, Onesimus, who had been converted and discipled by Paul in Rome.	***Date:*** c. AD 61 ***Recipients:*** Philemon at Colossae ***Origination:*** Paul's 1st Roman imprisonment

INTRODUCTION vv. 1–7	**BODY OF THE LETTER: PAUL'S APPEAL TO ACCEPT ONESIMUS vv. 8–20**			**CONCLUSION vv. 21–25**
Greetings of Grace vv. 1–3 **Paul's Prayers for Him vv. 4–7** Thanksgiving for His Love & Faith vv. 4–5 Confident Prayer for Greater Effectiveness vv. 6–7	**Paul's Friendly Approach in the Matter vv. 8–9**	**Paul's Appeal for Onesimus's Full Acceptance vv. 10–19** Onesimus's Story of Desertion & Conversion vv. 10–11 Onesimus's Return & Usefulness in Ministry vv. 12–13 Paul's Deference to Philemon v. 14 Argument from Providence to Receive Onesimus as a Partner vv. 15–17 Paul's Promise to Pay for Losses vv. 18–19	**Paul's Appeal to Their Friendship v. 20**	**Paul's Confidence in Philemon v. 21** **Paul's Travel Prospects v. 22** **Greetings from Rome vv. 23–24** **Final Blessing v. 25**

THE EPISTLE TO THE HEBREWS

The letter to the Hebrews has generated great debate amongst interpreters. Not only is the author unnamed but so are the recipients. As far back as the second century, copies of the letter bore the heading, "To the Hebrews." What seems clear is that the book is intended for professing Hebrew Christians who were tempted to revert to Judaism in order to escape persecution. The author eloquently exhorts his readers to retain their profession and confidence in Christ as Supreme Lord who is worthy of their worship and their suffering.

Many in the early centuries of the church believed Paul to be the author of the book, no doubt because of its reference to Timothy (13:23) and its many Pauline phrases. But many notable leaders objected to this ascription. Much of the style is different than Paul's more common Greek. Whoever the author was (and there are over a dozen proposals), he was clearly a part of Paul's ministry team and had connections with Rome (13:24). The recipients had a profound knowledge of the Old Testament and were facing persecution (12:4).

The viewpoint in the charts is that the author (not Paul) wrote to Jewish Christians in Rome facing persecution under Nero. Their temptation was to identify as Jews instead of Christians in order to evade hardship. The author challenges them that they cannot denigrate Christ and still claim Him. He is worthy not only of their trust but also their suffering. If this is correct, the letter could be dated c. AD 68, after Paul's martyrdom but before the Fall of Jerusalem in AD 70.

Another challenge is determining the book's structure. While the book ends like a letter (13:22–25), it begins and develops more like a sermon. Oratorical elements are so strong in the book that some have reconstructed a Greco-Roman rhetorical outline. Others have followed a simpler approach, noting the "better than" statements about Christs' supremacy. Still others believe they see a large-scale chiasm that organizes the book. The approach in the charts presents four major discourses that develop after the brief introduction (1:1–4).

The Initial Discourse details how Christ's mediatorial work is superior to the ministry of angels (1:5–2:18). Perhaps some of the Hebrews toyed with downplaying Jesus' identity to that of an angel. But Christ is distinctly better than all of them. The Historical Discourse shows how Christ was superior to Moses (3:1–41:3). Since Christ is divine and preexistent, he in essence built the house of worship in which Moses served. The author warns his readers not to be like the Israelites in Moses' day who perished in unbelief and did not enter God's rest. The culmination of God's rest is found in Jesus. The longest portion of the book is the Hard Discourse where the author demonstrates Christ to be superior to the Aaronic priestly system (4:14–10:18). Christ is the ultimate High Priest through whom man can finally and fully enter God's presence. His priesthood is distinct, being like that of the king-priest Melchizedek and endures forever. The Climactic Exhortation calls the readers to faithfulness in following Christ (10:19–12:27). They are invited to follow and warned not to discard Christ for their own sense of safety. Many Old Testament saints are presented as examples of those who suffered for their faith. God will reward endurance with an everlasting inheritance.

Finally, the extended conclusion encourages gratitude for gaining access by grace into God's kingdom and shows how that should demonstrate itself in daily living (12:28–13:35). An interchange of prayer requests and blessings closes out to book along with final words of greetings.

CHART 52
Hebrews

Purpose: The author eloquently exhorts his readers to retain their confession and confidence in Christ as Supreme Lord who is worthy of their worship and suffering, even in the face of mounting persecution and the temptation to revert to the legal safety of Judaism.

Date: Perhaps c. AD 64–68
Author: An unnamed associate of Paul's ministerial circle
Recipients: Jewish Christians, perhaps in Rome

INTRODUCTION 1:1–4	**BODY OF THE EXHORTATION 1:5–12:27**				**CONCLUSION 12:28–13:25**
God's Past Revelations thru the Prophets 1:1 **God's Ultimate Revelation in the Son 1:2** **Celebration of the Son's Surpassing Radiance & Sacrificial Success 1:3** **Transition to the Initial Discourse 1:4**	**INITIAL DISCOURSE: Christ's Mediation Superior to Angels' 1:5–2:18** *Introductory Texts:* Citation of OT Passages to Elevate the Son Above the Angels 1:5–14 *Exhortative Interlude:* The Danger of Neglecting Salvation So Great 2:1–4 *Concluding Argument:* Christ Humbled on Earth to Become Our Sacrifice & Surety of Glory 2:5–16 *Transition:* Pivot to the Historical Discourse 2:17–18	**HISTORICAL DISCOURSE: Christ's Mediation Superior to Moses' 3:1–4:13** *Introductory Argument:* Christ Built the House of God in Which Moses Merely Served 3:1–6 *Illustrative Caution:* Warning Against Following the Unbelief of Israel's First Generation 3:7–19 *Concluding Exhortation:* Call to Enter into God's Rest & Warning Against Rejection of Christ 4:1–13	**THE HARD DISCOURSE: Christ's Mediation Superior to the Aaronic System 4:14–10:18** *Introductory Exhortation:* Call to Draw Near to God through Christ, Our High Priest 4:14–16 *Opening Argument:* Jesus' Divine Appointment as Our Sympathetic High Priest 5:1–10 *Important Digression:* The Readers' Spiritual Impairments 5:11–6:20 *Argument Resumed:* Christ's Superior Mediatorial Work 7:1–10:18 Christ's Melchizedekian Priesthood 7:1–28 Christ's Initiation of the New Covenant 8:1–10:18 *The Supremacy of Christ's Heavenly Mediation 8:1–13* *The Supremacy of Christ's Blood Sacrifice 9:1–28* *The Fulfilling Satisfaction of Christ's Sacrifice 10:1–18*	**CLIMACTIC EXHORTATION: Call to Faithfulness in Following Christ 10:19–12:27** *Introductory Exhortation:* Call to Draw Near to God, Maintain Our Profession & Minister to One Another 10:19–25 *Grave Warning:* The Sorest of Punishments on Those Who Trample Christ Underfoot 10:26–31 *Curative Encouragement:* Reminder of Their Past Testimony and the Author's Confidence in Their Faith 10:32–39 *Historical Examples:* Saints of Old—and the Savior Himself—Who Lived by Faith in God's Promises 11:1–12:3 *Concluding Exhortation:* Endurance to be Rewarded with an Everlasting Inheritance 12:4–27	**Practical Implications 12:28–13:17** Call to Show Gratitude for Kingdom Inheritance 12:28–29 Thru Selfless Love & Living 13:1–6 Thru Obedient Identification with Christ & His People 13:7–17 **Concluding Interchange of Prayer 13:18–21** **Postscript 13:22–25**

CHART 53: Focus on Hebrews 1:5–4:13

INTRODUCTION, 1:1–4	BODY OF THE EXHORTATION, 1:5–12:27									CONCLUSION, 12:28–13:25
	INTRODUCTORY DISCOURSE: Christ's Mediation Superior to Angels' 1:5–2:18			**HISTORICAL DISCOURSE: Christ's Mediation Superior to Moses' 3:1–4:13**			THE HARD DISCOURSE: Christ's Mediation Superior to the Aaronic System, 4:14–10:18	CLIMACTIC EXHORTATION: Call to Faithfulness in Following Christ, 10:19–12:25		
	Introductory Texts: **Citation of OT Passages to Elevate the Son Above the Angels 1:5–14** *Psalm 2:7; 1 Samuel 7:14* 1:5 *Psalm 97:7* 1:6 *Psalm 104:4* 1:7 *Psalm 45:6–7* 1:8–9 *Psalm 102: 25–27* 1:10–12 *Psalm 110:1* 1:13 Concluding Contemplation on the Supporting Role of Angels 1:14	***Exhortative Interlude:*** **The Danger of Neglecting Salvation So Great 2:1–4** Warning to Not Drift Away from the Message 2:1 Illustration of Judgment Under the Law Which Angels Mediated 2:2 Lesser-to-Greater Comparison of Judgment on Those Rejecting Christ 2:3a Miraculous Attestation of Gospel to the First Generation of Christians 2:3b–4	***Concluding Argument:*** **Christ Humbled to Become Our Sacrifice & Surety of Glory 2:5–16** God's Plan for Man's Co-Regency in *Psalm 8:4–6* 2:5–8b Man's Failure 2:8c Jesus' Coming to Fulfill God's Plan 2:9 Christ's Sufferings 2:10–16 *According to God's Saving Plan 2:10* *Qualified Him to Represent Us 2:11–13* *Qualified Him to Redeem Us 2:14–16* ***Transition to Second Discourse:*** **The High Priestly Ministry of Jesus 2:17–18**	***Introductory Argument:*** **Christ Built the House of God in Which Moses Merely Served 3:1–6** The Call to Contemplate the Greatness of Jesus 3:1 Jesus is Far More Glorious than Moses 3:2–3 Comparison of Moses' Great Work & Christ's Greater Work with God's House 3:4–6a The Call to Hold Fast Their Confidence in Christ 3:6b	***Illustrative Caution:*** **Warning Against Following the Unbelief of Israel's First Generation 3:7–19** The Unbelief of Israel's First Generation Recounted in *Psalm 95* 3:7–11 *Exhortative Interlude:* Hold Fast to the End 3:12–15 The Judgment That Fell on the First Generation 3:16–19	***Concluding Exhortation:*** **Encouragement to Enter into God's Rest 4:1–13** Initial Call to Enter into God's Rest 4:1 Israel's First Generation Failed to Listen & Enter 4:2–3b God's Rest, a Sharing in His Pleasure with His People 4:3c–5 God's Shared Rest Still Available 4:6–10 Closing Call to Enter into God's Rest in Christ 4:11–13 *The Urgency of Entering 4:11* *Incisive Judgment Against Those Who Do Not Heed 4:12–13*				

CHART 54: Focus on Hebrews 4:14–10:18

INTRODUCTION, 1:1–4

BODY OF THE EXHORTATION, 1:5–12:27

INTRODUCTORY DISCOURSE: Christ's Mediation Superior to Angels', 1:5–2:18

HISTORICAL DISCOURSE: Christ's Mediation Superior to Moses', 3:1–4:13

THE HARD DISCOURSE: Christ's Mediation Superior to the Aaronic System, 4:14–10:18

Introductory Exhortation: **Call to Draw Near to God thru Christ, Our High Priest 4:14–16**	***Important Digression:*** **The Readers' Spiritual Impairments 5:11–6:20**	***Argument Resumed:*** **Christ's Superior Mediatorial Work 7:1–10:18**			
		Christ's Melchizedekian Priesthood 7:1–28	**Christ's Initiation of the New Covenant 8:1–10:18**		
Opening Argument: **Jesus' Divine Appointment as Our Sympathetic High Priest 5:1–10**			**The Supremacy of Christ's Heavenly Mediation 8:1–13**	**The Supremacy of Christ's Blood Sacrifice 9:1–28**	**The Fulfilling Satisfaction of Christ's Sacrifice 10:1–18**
The Sympathetic Nature of OT Priests Appointed by God 5:1–4	The Readers' Dullness of Hearing & Perception 5:11–14	Melchizedek's Priesthood a Higher Order than that of Aaron's 7:1–10	He is Our Intercessor in the Ultimate, Heavenly Sanctuary 8:1–6	The Sacred Rituals of the Old Sanctuary 9:1–10	The Old Sacrifices as Recurrent Shadows 10:1–4
Christ's Unique Appointment to the Melchizedekian Priesthood 5:5–6	Exhortation to Press on into Spiritual Maturity 6:1–3	The Need & God's Plan for a New Priesthood 7:11–14	He is Our Intercessor thru the New Covenant as *Jeremiah 31:31–34* Foretold 8:7–13	*The Sacred Implements 9:1–5*	Jesus' Destiny as God's Final Agent of Sanctification 10:5–10
Christ's Sufferings Used as Qualifiers for His Priestly Appointment 5:7–10	Dire Warning About the Point of No Return 6:4–8	The Divine Initiation of Jesus' Priesthood 7:15–19		*Daily Worship & the Day of Atonement 9:6–10*	Jesus' Sacrificial Work Completed Once for All 10:11–14
	Fiery Depiction of Loss 6:7–8	The Permanent & Perfect Priestly Ministry of Jesus 7:20–28		The Perfect Offering of Christ's Blood 9:11–14	The Spirit's Assurance of New Covenant Cleansing 10:15–18
	The Author's Positive Hopes for His Readers 6:9–12			Initiation of the New Covenant with His Blood 9:15–28	
	Confident Hope in God's Promises 6:13–20			*Christ's Death Initiated an Inheritance & Covenant 9:15–22*	
	The Example of Abraham's Confidence in God's Oath 6:13–16			*Christ's Death Accomplished Everlasting Cleansing 9:23–28*	
	The Encouragement of God's Oath Thru Jesus 6:17–20a				
	Transition Back to the Argument 6:20b				

CLIMACTIC EXHORTATION: Call to Faithfulness in Following Christ, 10:19–12:25

CONCLUSION, 12:28 –13:25

CHART 55: Focus on Hebrews 10:19–13:25

INTRODUCTION, 1:1–4

INTRODUCTORY DISCOURSE: Christ's Mediation Superior to Angels', 1:5–2:18

HISTORICAL DISCOURSE: Christ's Mediation Superior to Moses', 3:1–4:13

THE HARD DISCOURSE: Christ's Mediation Superior to the Aaronic System, 4:14–10:18

BODY OF THE EXHORTATION, 1:5–12:27

CLIMACTIC EXHORTATION: Call to Faithfulness in Following Christ, 10:19–12:25

Introductory Exhortation:
Call to Draw Near to God, Maintain Our Profession & Minister to One Another
10:19–25

Grave Warning:
The Sorest of Punishments on Those Who Trample Christ Underfoot
10:26–31

Curative Encouragement:
Remembrance of Their Past Testimony & the Author's Confidence in Their Faith
10:32–39

Historical Examples:
Saints of Old—and the Savior Himself—Who Lived by Faith in God's Promises
11:1–12:3

Introduction: Faith as the Basis of Hope throughout the Ages
11:1–3

The Faith of the Primeval Believers: Abel, Enoch & Noah
11:4–7

The Faith of Abraham & His Family
11:8–22

Sojourning in the Promised Land & Waiting for the Promised Heir
11:8–12

Interlude: *Amplification on the Faith of Sojourners*
11:13–16

Faith in God's Undying Promises throughout Generations
11:17–22

The Faith of Moses and His Associates
11:23–31

The Preservation & Earthly Separation of Moses
11:23–27

The Preservation & Early Success of the Nation
11:28–31

The Faith of Countless Other Ancient Saints Who Gained Victories and Endured Suffering by Faith
11:32–38

Summary: Encouragement to Emulate Ancient Faith
11:39–40

Finale: The Superior Example of Christ's Faith
12:1–3

Concluding Exhortation:
Endurance to be Rewarded with Everlasting Inheritance
12:4–27

The Call to Endure Suffering
12:4–11

Sufferings May Worsen
12:4

God's Loving, Fatherly Discipline
12:5–8

Sufferings are the Father's Formative Discipline
12:9–11

The Call to Help One Another in the Faith & Watch for Other's Souls
12:12–17

The Hope of Enjoying God in Heavenly Mt. Zion
12:18–24

The Awfulness of Approaching God on Mt. Sinai
12:18–21

The Blessedness of Approaching God in Heavenly Mt. Zion
12:22–24

Concluding Call to be Ready for the Great Final Shaking
12:25–27

CONCLUSION 12:28–13:25

Practical Implications
12:28–13:17

The Call to Show Gratitude for Kingdom Inheritance
12:28–29

Thru Selfless Love & Living
13:1–6

Thru Obedient Identification with Christ & His People
13:7–17

Following Godly Examples & Embracing Gospel Truths
13:7–9

Feasting on Christ & Sharing His Reproach
13:10–14

Worshiping God with Truly Spiritual Sacrifices
13:15–16

Following Godly Leadership
13:17

Concluding Interchange of Prayer
13:18–21

Postscript
13:22–25

THE EPISTLE OF JAMES

The epistle of James is likely the first New Testament Scripture inspired by the Spirit, written c. AD 45 to Jewish Christians in Palestine and Syria. The author who introduces himself in 1:1 is not the Apostle James but the half-brother of Jesus who became a key leader in the Jerusalem church. He died a martyr, stoned to death by the Sanhedrin in AD 62. No stranger to adversity in his earlier days, he writes this letter to help Jewish Christians pass the tests of their faith and grow in spiritual maturity. True faith leads one to actively heed God's word, carefully speak with others, and avoiding outburst of anger and arrogance.

The book reads like a collection of short messages that James has compiled for circulation. James' readers were experiencing all sorts of trials including sickness, persecution, exploitation, and temptations. His compiled messages provided comfort, counsel, and correction to those facing severe testing.

Though it is a small book, its interpretation has not been short of controversy. For instance, James' mention of Abraham being justified by his works and not by faith alone (2:22–24) has long been a proof text used against the Reformation—so much so that Martin Luther was uncomfortable with James' inclusion in Scripture. But James uses the word "justify" in a sense that means "shown to be righteous" as opposed to "declared to be righteous." Other interpretive cruxes abound in the book. Perhaps the most perplexing is determining its outline. Some don't believe there is any meaningful superstructure at all but see the book as the NT equivalent to Proverbs, renowned for its loosely connected maxims. Most interpreters see 12 or more distinct messages in the book.

The idea behind the chart is that 1:19b–21 is a proposition statement that provides a broad outline of the material that follows it. If this is correct, then 1:1–18 may be viewed as string of introductory exhortations about God's purposes for trials and temptations, culminating in the purpose statement about being "quick to hear, slow to speak, slow to anger" (v. 19). This counsel is relevant in many ways but is applied mostly to how one responds to God's Word. The first major segment of the body (1:22–2:26) corresponding with "quick to hear," stresses the need to heed God's word. God wants followers who not only hear but do His word. Such ones possess true religion that is self-controlled and self-giving, showing no partiality in dealing with others. This is the sort of faith that works, just like Abraham's.

The middle section (3:1–12), corresponding with "slow to speak," discusses the importance of careful, graceful speech with others. This immediately confronts the one who wishes to teach, for he must be mindful of the higher accountability to which God holds teachers. It applies to all Christians who need to remember the destructive potential of the tongue.

The final section (3:13–5:12), corresponding with "slow to anger," confronts the sin of anger and the arrogance often behind it. Those who claim to speak for God can become arrogant, but God's wisdom leads to peaceableness. The root behind sinful strife is the flesh, not the Spirit; it is a worldly orientation that requires repentance. The wealthy are prone to the arrogant abuse of their power, and James reminds them of their accountability to God. Those who suffer oppression are encouraged to humbly wait on the Lord, knowing that His reward is certain. The book's conclusion (5:13–20) calls the saints to prayerful care for one another.

CHART 56 **James** ©2015 M. Scott Bashoor	***Purpose***: James gathers a range of counsel for scattered Jewish Christians to help them grow in spiritual maturity and pass the tests of their faith. True faith leads one to actively heed God's Word, carefully speak with others, and avoid shows of anger and arrogance.	***Date:*** c. AD 45 ***Author:*** James, half-brother of Jesus and leader of the Jerusalem Church ***Recipients:*** Jewish Christians scattered abroad

INTRODUCTORY EXHORTATIONS **1:1–18**	**MAIN BODY** **1:19–5:12**						**CONCLUDING EXHORTATIONS** **5:13–20**
	ACTIVELY HEED GOD'S WORD **1:22–2:26**	**CAREFULLY SPEAK WITH OTHERS** **3:1–12**	**AVOID SHOWS OF ANGER AND ARROGANCE** **3:13–5:12**				
SALUTATION **1:1** **THE JOYFUL PURPOSE OF TRIALS** **1:2–12** Producing Virtue 1:2–4 Promoting Wisdom 1:5–8 Providing Perspective 1:9–12 **THE REAL DYNAMICS OF TEMPTATION** **1:13–18** God Not the Tempter 1:13–16 God, the Good Giver 1:17–18 **MAIN PROPOSITION: RESPONDING RIGHTLY TO THE ENGRAFTED WORD** **1:19–21**	**Doers of the Word** **1:22–25** **Marks of True Religion: Self-control & Self-giving** **1:26–27** **Practicing Impartiality** **2:1–13** Prejudice Against the Poor: Unjust & Unlike God 2:1–7 The Royal Law of Love: Gauge of Conduct & Judgment 2:8–13 **Faith Working with Works** **2:14–26** The Uselessness of Dead Faith 2:14 Illustration of Dead Faith: Indifference to the Needy 2:15–17 Answers to an Objector 2:18–20 Old Testament Illustrations 2:21–26	**Warning to Aspiring Teachers** **3:1–2a** **Warning on the Great Effect of the Tongue** **3:2b–5** **Warning on The Wickedness of the Tongue** **3:6–12** Humanly Untamable 3:6–8 Spiritually Duplicitous 3:9–10 Unnaturally Inconsistent 3:11–12	**God's Peaceable Wisdom** **3:13–18** The Gentleness of Wisdom 3:13 Marks of Worldly Wisdom 3:14–16 Marks of Heavenly Wisdom 3:17–18	**Warning on Worldly Strife** **4:1–12** The Carnal Root of Conflicts 4:1–3 An Indictment for Adultery with the World 4:4–5 A Call to Repentance 4:6–10 Unlawful Judging of One Another 4:11–12	**Warning on the Arrogance of Wealth** **4:13–5:6** Presump-tuous Planning Wealthy Christians Must Avoid 4:13–17 Fierce Judgment Oppressive Sinners Will Face 5:1–6 *Vision of Their Final Judgment* *5:1–3* *Indictment of Their Awful Exploitation* *5:4–6*	**Humble Endurance in the Face of Suffering** **5:7–12** The Call to Patience 5:7a Confidence in Final Reward 5:7b–8 Patience with Each Other in Times of Trial 5:9 The OT Record of Blessing on the Patient 5:10–11 Rejection of Oaths Even Under Pressure 5:12	**THE PLACE OF PRAYER IN VARIOUS TRIALS** **5:13–18** Prayers for All Occasions 5:13 Prayer of Faith for the Sick 5:14–15 Mutual Confession and Prayer 5:16 The Encouraging Example of Elijah 5:17–18 **EXHORTATION TO RESCUE ONE ANOTHER FROM SIN** **5:19–20**

THE EPISTLES OF PETER

In the last decade of the Apostle Peter's life, he wrote two epistles to Christians in five regions of Asia Minor. Peter apparently ministered in this area before moving to Rome alongside Mark (Acts 12:17; 1 Pet 5:13). The ethnic makeup of these churches is disputed, but Peter's descriptions of their backgrounds suggest they were Gentiles (1 Pet 1:14, 18; 2:9–10; 4:3). Peter heard how they were struggling under social pressure and persecution, and later he warns them of a wave of false teaching which would threaten their growth in Christ.

First Peter was written in c. AD 58–62 to encourage saints in hostile pagan lands to keep their hope in Christ's promises. They were to live holy lives despite mounting persecution and various trials which resulted in increasing alienation from their culture. Peter reminds them that though they're rejected by men, they have been chosen by God. As such, they should live holy lives in every area of life, looking for the final reward at Christ's coming.

The introduction (1:1–12) opens with a trinitarian greeting followed by a worshipful exposition of God's salvation, bringing hope and joy rooted in God's ancient revelations. The letter's first main segment (1:13–2:10) describes the newness of life initiated in salvation. Christians have entered a new life of hope and holiness, love and grace, and worship in God's new temple, the Church. The second section (2:11–4:11) teaches how Christian sojourning reorders relationships. Christians need an attitude of sojourning to relate properly to authorities and spouses. Relationships in a fallen world are complicated and call for a renewed inner life which can respond properly to suffering. The final section (4:12–5:11) encourages the saints to endure suffering for Christ's sake. God is faithful and His blessing is on those whom he proves in testing. The faithful Shepherd will lead his flock to final victory. The conclusion (5:12–14) passes on greetings, closing instructions, and exhortations to stand firm and maintain love.

Second Peter was written c. AD 67–68, to the same readers as 1 Peter. Peter's circumstances have changed as he is expecting martyrdom soon (1:12–15). The greatest threat to the churches was no longer persecution but a coming surge of false teaching through the region. The false teachers denied there would be a Second Coming and judgment to follow. This allowed them to create whatever immoral code of religious conduct they wished. Peter warns that judgment will indeed come. In the meantime, true believers are to grow in God's life-transforming grace. Peter ends by urging his readers to continue growing in the grace and knowledge of Christ so as to avoid grave spiritual derailments.

In the introduction (1:1–4), Peter prays for God's grace and peace to be multiplied in their lives. The first main section (1:5–21) is a call to grow in the grace and knowledge of Christ. Growth in virtue is the sensible outgrowth of saving grace. As an eyewitness to Jesus, the apostle stresses the urgency of following the glorious Christ. The middle section (2:1–22) exposes the spiritual threat of the false teachers (who were witnesses to nothing) and promises severe judgment for their carnality and hypocrisy. The final section (3:1–13) reminds them of prophecies of the Lord's coming. While the Lord's return may seem delayed, the Scriptures are clear that He is coming again in power and glory. In light of His swift return, Christians are called to live godly lives. The conclusion (3:14–18) leaves the readers with parting warnings of error and exhortations to grow in the grace and knowledge of Christ.

CHART 57 **1 Peter** ©2015 M. Scott Bashoor	***Purpose:*** Peter writes to Gentile Christians in hostile pagan lands to keep their hope on Christ's promises and to live a holy life before God despite mounting persecution and various trials.	***Date:*** c. AD 58–62 ***Recipients:*** Gentile Christians in NE Asia Minor ***Origination:*** Rome (aka "Babylon")

INTRODUCTION **1:1–12**	**BODY OF THE LETTER** **1:13–5:11**			**CONCLUSION** **5:12–14**
	LIVING THE NEWNESS OF LIFE INITIATED IN SALVATION **1:13–2:10**	**THE ORDERING OF RELATIONSHIPS FOR CHRISTIAN SOJOURNERS** **2:11–4:11**	**ENDURING THE ORDEAL OF SUFFERING FOR CHRIST'S SAKE** **4:12–5:11**	
Opening Salutation **1:1–2** **Expositional Praise for God's Salvation** **1:3–12** Hope in the Future Inheritance Yet to be Revealed 1:3–5 Joy in Present Sufferings that Purify the Believer 1:6–9 The Privilege of Past Revelations by the Prophets 1:10–12	**The New Life of Hope & Holiness in the Fear of the Lord** **1:13–21** Hope in Christ's Future Grace Leads to Practical Holiness 1:13–16 Regard for God's Saving Plan Leads to Accountable Living 1:17–21 **The New Life of Love & Grace in God's Family** **1:22–2:3** The New Life Enables a New Love for Others 1:22–25 The New Life Requires Ongoing Growth in Love 2:1–3 **The New Life of Worship & Welcome Before God** **2:4–10** Believers are Living Temple-Stones 2:4–8 Believers are New Covenant Priests 2:9–10	**Appeal to Christians as Sojourners** **2:11–12** **Submission & Honor to Governing Authorities** **2:13–17** **Submission & Honor to Slave masters: Honoring to God & Exemplified by Christ** **2:18–25** **Submission & Honor in Marriage** **3:1–7** **Inner Qualities for Relational Peace: Harmony, Humility, & Prayerful Trust** **3:8–12** **Godly Responses to Relational Suffering** **3:13–4:11** Trusting God When Suffering for Doing Right 3:13–14 Revering Christ as Lord with a Clear Conscience 3:15–17 Remembering Christ's Victory in Suffering 3:18–22 Committing to a Righteous Lifestyle in the World 4:1–6 Being Devoted to Brotherly Love in the Church 4:7–11	**The Blessing of Suffering for Righteousness's Sake** **4:12–16** **The Christian's Suffering as a Proving Judgment** **4:17–18** **The Trustworthiness of God in Sufferings** **4:19** **Christ's Shepherding of His Suffering Flock** **5:1–4** **The Final Exaltation of the Humble as Victors** **5:5–11** The Command to Humble Christian Relationships 5:5 The Call for Humble Trust in God 5:6–7 The Charge to Resist the Devil 5:8–9 The Confidence of Eternal Glory in the Everlasting Dominion 5:10–11	**Authorization of Silvanus as Peter's Messenger** **5:12a** **Call to Stand Firm in Grace** **5:12b** **Greetings from the Church in "Babylon" (Rome) & from Mark** **5:13** **Concluding Summons to Christian Love** **5:14a** **Farewell Prayer of Peace** **5:14b**

CHART 58 **2 Peter** ©2015 M. Scott Bashoor	***Purpose:*** Peter urges his readers to continue growing in the grace and knowledge of Christ to avoid the grave spiritual disruption threatened by a coming surge of false teachers and scoffers.			***Date:*** c. AD 67–68 ***Recipients:*** Perhaps Gentile Christians in Asia Minor ***Origination:*** Prison in Rome, nearing martyrdom
	BODY OF THE LETTER 1:5–3:13			
INTRODUCTION 1:1–4	**AN APOSTOLIC CALL TO GROW IN THE GRACE & KNOWLEDGE OF CHRIST 1:5–21**	**A DESCRIPTIVE WARNING ABOUT THE THREAT OF FALSE TEACHERS 2:1–22**	**AN IMPORTANT REMINDER ABOUT PROPHECIES OF THE LORD'S COMING 3:1–13**	**CONCLUSION 3:14–18**
Opening Salutation 1:1 **Confident Prayer that Grace & Peace Be Multiplied 1:2–4** Wish-Prayer for Grace & Peace 1:2 Based on God's Lavish Provision of Grace thru the Knowledge of Christ 1:3 Based on Christ's Precious Promises of Transformation & Deliverance 1:4	**A Sensible Call to Grow in Grace-Based Virtues 1:5–11** The Diligent Development of a Godly Life Rooted in Grace 1:5–7 The Enabling & Confirming Value of Virtues Rooted in Grace 1:8–11 *Greater Usefulness & Fruitfulness 1:8–9* *Confirmation of Kingdom Access 1:10–11* **An Apostolic Reminder of the Glorious Truth of Christ 1:12–21** Peter's Personal Urgency in Spurring on Their Godliness 1:12–15 Peter's Personal Remembrance of Christ's Divine Glory 1:16–18 The Prophetic Confirmation of the Glorious Truth of Christ 1:19–21	**The Coming Surge of False Teachers 2:1–3a** **The Coming Judgment on False Teachers 2:3b–10a** Judgment is Already Brewing 2:3b Three Notable Past Judgments & Deliverances 2:4–8 Confidence in Future Judgment & Deliverance 2:9–10a **Vivid Description of Their Proud Rebellion, Revelry & Carnality 2:10b–16** Foolishly Playing with Spirits, Like Dumb Beasts 2:10b–13a Foolishly Captivated by Carnality, Like Balaam, the Dumb Priest 2:13b–16 **Their Emptiness & Worsened Estate 2:17–22** Their Empty Promises Exposed 2:17–19 Their Gloomy Future Explained 2:20–22	**Divine Revelation of the Lord's Coming 3:1–7** A Reminder of the Teaching of the Prophets of Old & Christ's Apostles 3:1–2 The Need for the Reminder: The Upsurge of Scoffers 3:3–7 *A Summary of Their Sensual Scoffings 3:3–4* *Their Forgetfulness of the Famous Flood 3:5–7* **The Divine Plan & the Seeming Delay of the Lord's Return 3:8–10** God's Reckoning of Time 3:8 God's Patience Before Judgment 3:9 The Consummation Still Swift & Final 3:10 **Call to Godly Living in Light of the Fast-Coming End 3:11–13**	**Call to Live Blamelessly, Waiting for the Lord's Coming 3:14–15a** **Confirmation from Paul's Teaching 3:15b–16a** **Warning about False Teachers' Distortions 3:16b–17** **Call to Grow in the Grace & Knowledge of Christ 3:18a** **Christ-Centered Doxology 3:18b**

THE EPISTLES OF JOHN

The epistles of John reflect his pastoral concern for churches and church leaders in western Asia Minor where he exercised apostolic authority in the final decades of his life (see the introduction to John's Gospel). He was greatly concerned about the recent spread of false Christian movements, perhaps versions of proto-Gnosticism. John is equally passionate about encouraging the saints and the gospel ministry. He wrote all three letters from Ephesus between AD 80–90, but it is unclear the order in which they were written. Unlike other NT letters intended as sequels, none of these three shares precisely the same audience.

First John is written to believers whose churches had recently suffered schism at the hands of false teachers. John encourages the saints with assuring truths, calling them to keep the Christian path of life and love. The churches had been invaded by a surge of false teachers who claimed to have a special knowledge of God. They developed a following of defectors who eventually withdrew from the churches, leaving the faithful to wonder whether they were the unenlightened ones (2:18–21).

John's spiraled writing style has perplexed interpreters' attempts to discern his flow of thought. The outline in the chart sees three overlapping movements which assure the believers that they truly know the God of light, love, and righteousness. After the introduction in which John asserts his eyewitness testimony (1:1–4), the first movement counters the false teachers' claim that they specially understood the divine (1:5–2:27). Those who truly walk in the light of the gospel—unlike the errorists—have a consciousness of sin, and value the Savior's sin-cleansing blood. They hear the call to obey God's commands including the greatest commandment, love. The recent unloving schism was the work of "anti-Christs," but the faithful remnant had real spiritual insight.

The second movement assures believers they are in fellowship with the God of righteousness (2:28–4:6). True children of God desire to be ready for the Lord's coming, forsaking sin and the devil's work. Because the world is such a hateful place, it is essential that believers love one another. Knowing the God of righteousness leads them to reject the worldly errors of false religion.

The final movement stresses strongly the loving nature of God and his fellowship (4:7–5:12). Love is essential to God's character and those who are in His fellowship. As believers emulate God's love, their confidence before Him grows as they demonstrate the victorious faith they have. God's own loving witness to Christ encourages believers to embrace love as a fundamental of their faith.

The letter's conclusion asserts John's purpose for writing—assurance—and counsels them in intercessory prayer, while stressing the need for gospel certainty in days of defection (5:13–21).

Second John is written to a "chosen lady" (either a key woman who hosts a house-church, or a euphemism for a local church) to encourage hospitality for Christian workers and to reject false workers. John commends the spiritual growth of the lady's children (either literal children, or members of the church), and encourages them to continue their service for Christ and the care of traveling Christian workers. John warns them not to extend hospitality to false teachers lest they end up partaking in their evil deeds.

Third John is written to a church leader named Gaius to commend his continued hospitality for godly Christian workers despite the selfish opposition of Diotrephes, a defiant church leader who rejected John's authority. John's letter publicly commends Gaius and condemns Diotrephes, preparing the way for John's visit when he would personally straighten out matters in their church.

CHART 59 **1 John** ©2015 M. Scott Bashoor	***Purpose:*** John writes to believers whose churches had recently suffered schism at the hands of false teachers advocating another path to knowing God. John encourages them with assuring truths, calling them to keep to the Christian path of life and love.	***Date:*** c. AD 80–90 ***Recipients:*** Gentile Christians in western Asia Minor ***Origination:*** Ephesus

INTRODUCTION 1:1–4	**BODY OF THE LETTER 1:5–5:12**			**CONCLUSION 5:13–21**
	ASSURANCES OF FELLOWSHIP WITH THE GOD OF LIGHT 1:5 –2:27	**ASSURANCES OF FELLOWSHIP WITH THE GOD OF RIGHTEOUSNESS 2:28–4:6**	**ASSURANCES OF FELLOWSHIP WITH THE GOD OF LOVE 4:7–5:12**	
Opening Testimony on Eternal Life 1:1–3a John was a Firsthand Witness of Christ 1:1 God has Truly Manifested Life in His Son 1:2 John is Truly God's Messenger 1:3a **Initial Statements of Purpose 1:3b–4** To Promote the Lord's Fellowship 1:3b To Increase Mutual Joy 1:4	**Walking in God's Light with a Consciousness of Sin & Cleansing 1:5–10** **Obeying God's Commandments & Overcoming Evil 2:1–17** Avoiding Sin & Claiming Propitiation 2:1–2 Obedience an Indicator of Knowing God 2:3–6 Obedience Illustrated in Loving Others 2:7–11 Victory for Every Stage of the Christian Life 2:12–14 Victory Over the Soon-Passing World 2:15–17 **Avoiding the Anti-Christs' Errors 2:18–27** The Recent Schism Explained as the Work of Anti-Christs 2:18–21 The Pseudo-Spiritual Denial of Christ 2:22–24 The True Spiritual Insight of Believers 2:25–27	**Living as Children of God 2:28–3:10** Readiness for the Lord's Coming 2:28–3:3 Forsaking Sin & the Devil's Work 3:4–10 **Loving God's Family in a Hateful World 3:11–24** Lessons of Love and Hate from the Example of Cain 3:11–15 Sacrificial Love for the Brethren 3:16–18 Love & Obedience a Confirming Evidence of Fellowship with God 3:19–24 **Rejecting Worldly Religious Error 4:1–6** The Call to Discernment of Spiritualistic Teachings 4:1–3 The Believer's Reception of Apostolic Teaching 4:4–6	**Embracing Love as Essential to God's Character & Christian Faith 4:7–5:5** God's Inherent Love Made Manifest & Emulated by Believers 4:7–12 Confidence Before God Gained by Perfecting of Love for God in Christ 4:13–18 God's Initiative of Love & the Christian's Loving Response 4:19–21 Victorious Faith Demonstrated in Love for God's Children & God's Son 5:1–5 **Embracing God's Love Encouraged by God's Own Witness to Christ 5:6–12** God's Historical & Spiritual Witness 5:6–8 God's External & Internal Witness 5:9–10 God's Evangelical & Essential Witness 5:11–12	**Concluding Statement of Purpose: Gaining Certainty of Eternal Life 5:13** **Counsel for the Believer's Prayer Life 5:14–17** Confidence Before God 5:14–15 Intercession for Those in Error 5:16–17 **Certainty in the Cosmic Struggle of Truth & Error 5:18–20** **Concluding Call to Flee Idols (False Faiths) 5:21**

CHART 60 **2 John** ©2015 M. Scott Bashoor	***Purpose:*** John encourages an unnamed church and its members (or woman and her children) to continue practicing love and hospitality but not to give physical or emotional support to the many false teachers traveling through the area.	***Date:*** c. AD 80–90 ***Recipients:*** An unnamed "lady" and her "children" ***Origination:*** Ephesus, leading city of Asia Minor

INTRODUCTION **vv. 1–4**	**BODY OF THE LETTER** **vv. 5–11**			**CONCLUSION** **vv. 12–13**
Salutation **vv. 1–3** John's Self-Identification as "The Elder" v. 1a The Recipients: An Unnamed Church & Her Members v. 1b Conveyance of Christian Love vv. 1c–2 Greetings of Grace, Mercy & Peace v. 3 **Commendation of Faithful Members John Had Met** **v. 4**	**Reminder of the Fundamental Command to Show Love** **vv. 5–6** Not a New Command but Original to the Faith v. 5 Love for God & Its Resultant Obedience v. 6a Not New to the Readers but Original to Their Christian Experience v. 6b	**Caution about Becoming Entangled with False Teachers** **vv. 7–9** Many Antichrist Teachers Afoot v. 7 Christians to Beware of Losing Reward thru Entanglement v. 8 Deniers of Christ Cast as Devoid of God v. 9	**Command Not To Show Hospitality to False Teachers** **vv. 10–11** No Material or Emotional Support Permitted v. 10 Support of Errorists Cast as Fellowship with Evil v. 11	**Statement of Intent to Visit for Further Ministry** **v. 12** **Farewell Greetings from Members of a Sister Church** **v. 13**

CHART 61 3 John ©2015 M. Scott Bashoor	***Purpose:*** John writes to Gaius to commend and encourage his continued hospitality and support of godly Christian workers despite the selfish opposition of Diotrephes, a church leader who rejects John's authority.			***Date:*** c. AD 80–90 ***Recipients:*** A church leader named Gaius ***Origination:*** Ephesus, leading city of Asia Minor	
INTRODUCTION vv. 1–4	**BODY OF THE LETTER vv. 5–12**			**CONCLUSION vv. 13–15**	
Author: John's Self-identification as "The Elder" v. 1a **Recipient: Gaius, a Well-loved Disciple v. 1b** **Prayer for His Complete Wellbeing v. 2** **Joy Over a Commendation of Gaius from Traveling Brothers vv. 3–4**	**Commendation of Gaius for His Ministry of Hospitality vv. 5–8** Hospitality Ministry a Notable Aspect of His Faithfulness v. 5 Traveling Christians' Testimony of Gaius' Hospitality v. 6a The Care of Christian Workers for Their Sacrificial Service vv. 6b–7 The Ministry of Hospitality as a Christian Obligation & Opportunity v. 8	**Rebuke of Diotrephes for His Rebellious Leadership vv. 9–10** His Self-Exaltation & Rejection of John's Leadership v. 9 John's Plan to Correct Him Publicly v. 10	**Commendation of Godly Examples vv. 11–12** Call to Shun Bad Examples & Imitate Good Examples v.11a Commendation of Doers of Good, Indictment of Evildoers v. 11b–c Commendation of Demetrius (Perhaps the Messenger) v. 12	**Statement of Intent to Visit for Further Ministry vv. 13–14** **Farewell Prayer of Peace v. 15a** **Final Exchange of Greetings v. 15b**	

THE EPISTLE OF JUDE

This short epistle is written by Jude, the brother of James and half-brother of Jesus (Jude 1; cf. James 1:1). Much of the letter is identical or similar to the central section of 2 Peter. It has long been debated whether Peter borrowed from Jude, Jude borrowed from Peter, or whether they both borrowed from some other apostolic teaching. The fact that Jude is shorter than 2 Peter, while suggestive, does not prove the latter is an expansion of the smaller work. One difference between the two is that while Peter describes a coming wave of false teachers (2 Pet 3:3), Jude speaks of the surge as already present (Jude 17). If this reading is correct, Jude may be directed to the same audience of martyred Peter (c. AD 68–69). He wrote to churches beleaguered by an invasion of false teachers, urging Christians to contend for the truth of the Faith revealed through the apostles (Jude 3). Jude highlights the depravity of the false teachers who denied the Lord's coming and final judgment, showing how they were destined for great judgment. While the letter is mostly an exposé of error, it opens and closes with precious promises of God's preservation of His people (vv. 1, 24–25).

CHART 62 **Jude** ©2015 M. Scott Bashoor	***Purpose:*** Jude writes to churches beleaguered by an invasion of false teachers, urging them to contend for the faith as revealed thru the apostles and to build themselves up in the faith and God's love.	***Date:*** Perhaps c. AD 68–80 ***Recipients:*** Perhaps the same as 1 and 2 Peter ***Author:*** Jude, brother of James, half-brother of Jesus

INTRODUCTION vv. 1–4	**BODY OF THE LETTER vv. 5–23**			**CONCLUSION vv. 24–25**
	THE FALSE TEACHERS DESCRIBED IN TERMS OF THEIR CARNAL CHARACTER & ULTIMATE JUDGMENT 1:5–16		**THE AFFECTED BELIEVERS INSTRUCTED IN MAINTAINING THE FAITH & MINISTERING TO THE ERRANT vv. 17–23**	
Opening Salutation v. 1 **Prayer for God's Multiplied Mercy, Peace & Love v. 2** **Purpose Statement of the Letter vv. 3–4** The Original Intent to Encourage Changed to Give Urgent Exhortation v. 3 The Change Required by an Incursion of Dangerous False Teachers v. 4	**Reminder of the Judgment of God vv. 5–10** Three Examples of God's Judgment in History vv. 5–7 *Unbelievers after the Exodus v. 5* *Fallen Angels v. 6* *Sodom & Gomorrah v. 7* Three of the False Teachers' Sins Demanding God's Judgment vv. 8–10 *Three Sins Enumerated as Defilement, Rebellion & Revilement of the Spirit World v. 8* *Their Revilement Contrasted with Michael's Contest with Satan v. 9* *Their Similarities with Unthinking Beasts v. 10*	**Judgment to Fall on the False Teachers vv. 11–16** Declaration of Woe v. 11a Their Worthiness of Judgment vv. 11b–13 *Likened to Cain, Balaam & Korah v. 11b* *Likened to Dangerous Reefs, Waterless Clouds, Dead Trees, Wild Waves & Wandering Stars vv. 12–13* The Prophecy of Enoch Against the Ungodly vv. 14–15 Closing Character Indictment of the False Teachers v. 16	**Reminder of the Apostolic Instruction vv. 17–19** The Apostolic Prophecy of the Surge of Carnal Scoffers vv. 17–18 Application of the Prophecy to the False Teachers v. 19 **Call to Perseverance in God's Love thru Edification, Prayer & Hope in Christ's Coming vv. 20–21** **Call to a Ministry of Mercy to Those Impacted by the False Teachers vv. 22–23**	**Concluding Doxology vv. 24–25** Praise to God Who Gives Stability in Life & Standing in Glory v. 24 Eternal Praise to God Offered thru Christ v. 25

THE REVELATION OF JOHN

The Apostle John's final work constitutes a unique contribution to New Testament literature. The Book of Revelation contains elements which are epistolary (especially chap. 2–3), and the whole work was circulated along an imperial route to seven churches in Asia Minor. But most of the book contains a transcription of startling visions given to John while he was a prisoner for the faith on the island of Patmos. Traditionally the date for this work has been set between AD 90–96 during the reign of Emperor Domitian. John records four great visions given by Jesus Christ about events in the life of the church and the end of the age. He encourages and challenges believers to turn away from sin and continue in faithfulness in light of future judgments and final glory.

Despite the pastoral aim of the book, the book has become a battleground for interpretive approaches. The charts follow a futurist perspective which sees much prophetic imagery in the book pertaining to the end of days. The structure of Revelation is also greatly disputed. That the first segment is chapters 1–3 is generally accepted, but the proper division of the remainder has eluded consensus. Some understand Jesus' words in 1:19 as indicative of an outline focusing on the vision of Jesus ("things which you have seen," chap. 1), concerns for the first century church ("things which are," chap. 2–3), and matters pertaining to the eschaton ("things which will take place," chap. 4–22). While the book certainly covers these issues, that outlining can result in a somewhat imbalanced structure. For example, the sections most directly addressed to the early church (chap. 2–3) contain prophecies of the future, and the futuristic section contains descriptions of the past and present (e.g., chap. 12).

Another approach sees the book unfold in seven acts, each marked by seven enumerated items: seven lamps (1:9–3:22), seven seals (4:1–8:4), seven trumpets (8:5–11:18), seven scenes (11:19–15:4), seven bowls (15:5–16:21), seven judgments (17:1–20:3), and seven promises (20:4–22:5). John's penchant for sevens is obvious, but it is not so obvious that this is the defining matrix of the book. Yet another approach reads the book as a giant chiasm, expanding and retracting in counter-balancing sections. The center of this X-pattern is "the great sign" of the Child and the dragon (12:1–17). While chiasms are an undeniable literary tool of some biblical writers, that they are used as macro-structural tools for composition remains unconvincing.

The outlines are keyed into four statements about John "seeing" visions while "in the Spirit," a combination which occurs at the beginning of each major scene. The first vision (1:9–3:22) is of the ascended Christ and His word to the seven churches. The second vision (4:1–16:21) reveals the heavenly throne room and the coming great tribulation. The third vision (17:1–21:8) unveils the coming King, His millennial reign, and the final judgment. The final vision (21:9–27) previews the new creation and the eternal state. This four-fold arrangement explains some of the repetitions in the book. For instance, 21:1–8 introduces the new heaven and earth (vision 3) which is reintroduced in 22:1–5 (vision 4). One criticism of this approach is that chapters 4–16 seem outsized compared to the other sections. But this is offset by several interludes which divide and subdivide vision 2 (7:1–17; 10:1–11:14, and especially 12:1–14:20) which is situated in the middle of the book.

The book concludes with a four-fold cluster of interchanges between John and Jesus (22:6–21). The radiant Christ utters His final inscripturated words to the church and the world, calling all to be ready for His immanent return. With John's final assertion of Jesus' grace, the biblical canon closes.

CHART 63 **Revelation** ©2015 M. Scott Bashoor	***Purpose:*** John records four great visions given by Jesus Christ about events in the life of the church and the end times. He encourages and challenges believers to turn away from sin and continue in faithfulness in light of future judgments and final glory.	***Date:*** c. AD 90–96 ***Recipients:*** Seven churches in western Asia Minor ***Origination:*** Imprisoned on the isle of Patmos

INTRODUCTION: John's Greeting & Christ's Opening Words 1:1–8	**BODY OF THE BOOK: FOUR HEAVENLY VISIONS 1:9–22:5**				**CONCLUSION: John's Invitation & Christ's Final Words 22:6–21**
	THE FIRST VISION: The Ascended Christ & the Seven Churches 1:9–3:22	**THE SECOND VISION: The Throne Room & the Great Tribulation 4:1–16:21**	**THE THIRD VISION: The Coming King & Final Judgments 17:1–21:8**	**THE FOURTH VISION: The New Creation & the Eternal State 21:9–22:5**	
Prologue 1:1–3 **Greetings of Grace 1:4–5a** **Doxology 1:5b–6** **Introductory Oracles 1:7–8** Daniel's Prophecy of Christ's Coming 1:7 Christ's Announcement of His Presence 1:8	**Christ's Burning Glory Amidst the Seven Lampstands 1:9–20** **Christ's Dictated Letters to the Seven Churches 2:1–3:22** To Ephesus 2:1–7 To Smyrna 2:8–11 To Pergamum 2:12–17 To Thyatira 2:18–29 To Sardis 3:1–6 To Philadelphia 3:7–13 To Laodicea 3:14–22	**The Throne Room & the Seven Seals 4:1–8:1** The Heavenly Throne Room 4:1–5:14 The Opening of the Seven Seals 6:1–8:1 **Warnings of Wrath & the Seven Trumpets 8:2–11:19** Heavenly Fire Cast Down 8:2–6 The Blasts of the Seven Trumpets 8:7–11:19 **INTERLUDE: The Cosmic Conflict 12:1–14:20** The Satanic Plan & Heaven's Response 12:1–13:18 The Divine Plan & Heaven's Victory 14:1–20 **The Plague Judgments of the Seven Bowls 15:1–16:21** Heaven's Preparation for Judgment 15:1–8 The Pouring Out of the Seven Bowls 16:1–21	**The Fall of Babylon & the Victory of the Lamb 17:1–19:10** Babylon Depicted as a Great Harlot on a Scarlet Beast 17:1–18 The Great Fall of Babylon 18:1–24 Heaven's Celebration 19:1–10 **The Kingdom Come & the Consummation of History 19:11–21:8** Christ's Victorious Return & Millennial Reign 19:11–20:6 The Final Rebellion & Final Judgment 20:7–15 The New Heaven & the New Earth 21:1–8	**The New Jerusalem: The Eternal Temple 21:9–27** Description of the City's Surpassing Beauty 21:9–21 Description of the City's Consummate Holiness 21:22–27 **The New Heaven & the New Earth: Paradise Restored 22:1–5** The River of Life & the Tree of Life 22:1–2 The Elimination of the Curse & the Night 22:3–5	**First Round of Christ's Final Words 22:6–9** **Second Round of Christ's Final Words 22:10–15** **Third Round of Christ's Final Words 22:16–17** **Fourth Round of Christ's Final Words 22:18–21**

CHART 64: Focus on Revelation 1:9–3:22

INTRODUCTION, 1:1–8

BODY OF THE BOOK: FOUR HEAVENLY VISIONS, 1:9–22:5

THE FIRST VISION: THE ASCENDED CHRIST & THE SEVEN CHURCHES 1:9–3:22

Christ's Burning Glory Amidst the Seven Lampstands 1:9–20	Christ's Dictated Letters to the Seven Churches 2:1–3:22						
	Letter to Ephesus 2:1–7	**Letter to Smyrna 2:8–11**	**Letter to Pergamum 2:12–17**	**Letter to Thyatira 2:18–29**	**Letter to Sardis 3:1–6**	**Letter to Philadelphia 3:7–13**	**Letter to Laodicea 3:14–22**
The Setting on Patmos 1:9–10a Christ's Voice Heard 1:10b–11 Christ's Glory Seen 1:12–17 *Setting of the Seven Lampstands 1:12* *Description of the Glorified Christ 1:13–16* *John's Collapse 1:17a* Christ's Speech to John 1:17b–20 *Christ's Rehabilitation of John 1:17b* *Christ's Self-Introduction 1:18* *The Command to Write 1:19* *Interpretation of the Stars & Lampstands 1:20*	Address & Descript-ion of Christ 2:1 Affirm-ation 2:2–3 Rebuke 2:4 Warning of Christ's Coming & Call to Repent 2:5 Affirm-ation 2:6 Call to Listen 2:7a Eschato-logical Promise for Victors 2:7b	Address & Description of Christ 2:8 Affirm-ation 2:9 Assurance of Christ's Coming 2:10 Call to Listen 2:11a Eschato-logical Promise for Victors 2:11b	Address & Description of Christ 2:12 Affirmation 2:13 Rebuke 2:14–15 Warning of Christ's Coming & Call to Repent 2:16 Call to Listen 2:17a Eschato-logical Promise for Victors 2:17b	Address & Description of Christ 2:18 Affirmation 2:19 Rebuke 2:20–21 Warning of Christ's Coming & Call to Repent 2:22–23 Affirmation 2:24 Eschato-logical Promise for Victors 2:25–28 Call to Listen 2:29	Address & Description of Christ 3:1a Rebuke 3:1b–2 Warning of Christ's Coming & Call to Repent 3:3 Affirmation 3:4 Eschato-logical Promise for Victors 3:5 Call to Listen 3:6	Address & Description of Christ 3:7 Affirmation 3:8 Assurance of Christ's Coming 3:9–11 Eschatological Promise for Victors 3:12 Call to Listen 3:13	Address & Descrip-tion of Christ 3:14 Rebuke 3:15–17 Warning of Christ's Coming & Call to Repent 3:18–20 Eschato-logical Promise for Victors 3:21 Call to Listen 3:22

THE SECOND VISION, 4:1–16:21

THE THIRD VISION, 17:1–21:8

THE FOURTH VISION, 21:9–22:5

CONCLUSION, 22:6–21

CHART 65: Focus on Revelation 4:1–11:19

INTRODUCTION, 1:1–8	THE FIRST VISION, 1:9–3:22	BODY OF THE BOOK: FOUR HEAVENLY VISIONS, 1:9–22:5						INTERLUDE: The Cosmic Conflict, 12:1–14:20	The Plague Judgments of the Seven Bowls, 15:1–16:21	THE THIRD VISION, 17:1–21:8	THE FOURTH VISION, 21:9–22:5	CONCLUSION, 22:6–21
		THE SECOND VISION: THE THRONE ROOM & THE GREAT TRIBULATION, 4:1–16:21										
		The Throne Room & the Seven Seals 4:1–8:1		Warnings of Wrath & the Seven Trumpets 8:2–11:19								
					The Blasts of the Seven Trumpets 8:6–11:19							
		The Heavenly Throne Room 4:1–5:14 The Throne Surrounded by Twenty-Four Elders 4:1–4 The Four Creatures Who Lead in Divine Worship 4:5–11 The Book with Seven Seals 5:1–4 The Worthiness of the Lion Who Is the Lamb 5:5–14	**The Opening of the Seven Seals 6:1–8:1** The Six Seals of Judgment Opened 6:1–17 *The 1st Seal: White Horse of Conquest 6:1–2* *The 2nd Seal: Red Horse of Mutual Destruction 6:3–4* *The 3rd Seal: Black Horse of Famine 6:5–6* *The 4th Seal: Pale Horse of Many Perils 6:7–8* *The 5th Seal: Martyrs Under the Altar 6:9–11* *The 6th Seal: Cosmological Terror 6:12–17* INTERLUDE: The Two Redeemed Multitudes 7:1–17 *144,000 Redeemed from Israel 7:1–8* *The Multitude of Gentile Believers 7:9–17* The 7th Seal of Judgment Opened: Silence in Heaven for Half an Hour 8:1	**Heavenly Fire Cast Down 8:2–6** Distribution of Seven Trumpets to Seven Angels 8:2 A Burning Censer Cast to Earth from Heaven 8:3–5 The Angels Prepare to Blow 8:6	**Blast of the First Six Trumpets 8:7–9:21** The 1st Trumpet: Death to Vegetation 8:7 The 2nd Trumpet: Death in the Sea 8:8–9 The 3rd Trumpet: Death in Fresh Waters 8:10–11 The 4th Trumpet: Dimming of Heavenly Lights 8:12–13 The 5th Trumpet: Tormenting Spirits Unleashed—the 1st Woe 9:1–12 *Tormenting Locusts from the Bottomless Pit 9:1–6* *The Locusts' Frightful Description 9:7–12* The 6th Trumpet: Deadly Armies Unleashed—The 2nd Woe 9:13–21	**INTERLUDE: The Little Book & the Two Witnesses 10:1–11:14** The Little Book 10:1–11 *Presentation of the Book with Thunder 10:1–7* *The Bittersweet Taste of the Scroll 10:8–11* The 2 Witnesses 11:1–14 *Measuring of the Defiled Temple 11:1–2* *Judgment from the 2 Witnesses 11:3–6* *Their Martyrdom & Resurrection 11:7–13* *The 3rd Woe Introduced 11:14*	**Blast of the Seventh Trumpet 11:15–19** Acclamation of Christ as Conquering King 11:15–18 The Heavenly Temple Opened & God's Presence Manifest 11:19					

CHART 66: Focus on Revelation 12:1–16:21

INTRODUCTION, 1:1–8

BODY OF THE BOOK: FOUR HEAVENLY VISIONS, 1:9–22:5

THE FIRST VISION, 1:9–3:22

THE SECOND VISION:
THE THRONE ROOM & THE GREAT TRIBULATION
4:1–16:21

The Throne Room & the Seven Seals, 4:1–8:1

Warnings of Wrath & the Seven Trumpets, 8:2–11:19

INTERLUDE: The Cosmic Conflict 12:1–14:20

The Satanic Plan & Heaven's Response 12:1–13:18

Introduction to the Woman, the Dragon & the Child: Satan's Threat to Baby Jesus 12:1–6

The Dragon's War in Heaven: Michael's Victory Over Evil Forces 12:7–12

The Dragon's War on Earth: His Thwarted Attempt to Destroy the Woman 12:13–17

The Two Destructive Beasts 13:1–18

The Beast Arising from the Sea: The Antichrist 13:1–10

The Beast Arising from the Land: The False Prophet 13:11–18

The Divine Plan & Heaven's Victory 14:1–20

The Lamb's 144,000 & Their Song 14:1–5

The Six Commissioned Angels 14:6–20

The Message of Three Angels: The Fall of Babylon & Judgment to Come 14:6–13

The Reaping of Three Angels: The Sickling of the Earth & Treading of the Winepress 14:14–20

The Plague Judgments of the Seven Bowls 15:1–16:21

Heaven's Preparation for Judgment 15:1–16:1

Preparation of the Seven Plagues 15:1

Heavenly Victors Sing the Song of Moses 15:2–4

Seven Angels Given Seven Bowls of Wrath 15:5–8

The Command to Pour the Bowls 16:1

The Pouring Out of the Seven Bowls 16:2–21

The Pouring of the First Six Bowls 16:2–12

The First Bowl: Boils 16:2

The Second Bowl: Sea Turned to Blood 16:3

The Third Bowl: Freshwaters Turned to Blood 16:4–7

The Fourth Bowl: Scorching Heat 16:8–9

The Fifth Bowl: Darkness 16:10–11

The Sixth Bowl: The Parching of Euphrates 16:12

INTERLUDE: The Evil Gathering at Armageddon 16:13–16

The Pouring of the Seventh Bowl: The Great Shaking & the Fall of Babylon 16:17–21

THE THIRD VISION, 17:1–21:8

THE FOURTH VISION, 21:9–22:5

CONCLUSION, 22:6–21

CHART 67: Focus on Revelation 17:1–21:8

INTRODUCTION, 1:1–8

BODY OF THE BOOK: FOUR HEAVENLY VISIONS, 1:9–22:5

THE FIRST VISION, 1:9–3:22

THE SECOND VISION, 4:1–16:21

THE THIRD VISION:
THE JUDGMENTS & KINGDOM AT CHRIST'S SECOND COMING
17:1–21:8

The Fall of Babylon & the Victory of the Lamb 17:1–19:10			**The Kingdom Come & the Consummation of History 19:11–21:8**		
Babylon Depicted as a Great Harlot on a Scarlet Beast 17:1–18	**The Great Fall of Babylon 18:1–24**	**Heaven's Celebration 19:1–10**	**Christ's Victorious Return & Millennial Reign 19:11–20:6**	**The Final Rebellion & Final Judgment 20:7–15**	**The New Heaven & the New Earth 21:1–8**
The Startling Description of Woman on the Beast 17:1–6 The Vision of the Woman & Beast Explained 17:7–18 *The Beast, the Seven Heads & the Ten Horns 17:7–13* *The Victory of the Lamb Over the Evil Forces 17:14–18*	Angelic Announcement of Babylon's Fall 18:1–3 Angelic Warning of Babylon's Fall 18:4–20 *Call for the Righteous to Flee Babylon 18:4–8* *Three Woes from Babylon's Partners 18:9–19* *Summons for Heaven to Rejoice at God's Vindicating Judgment 18:20* The Certainty of Babylon's Downfall 18:21–24	Four-Fold Hallelujah for Babylon's Fall 19:1–6 The Marriage Supper of the Lamb 19:7–10	The Destruction of the Beast, the False Prophet & Their Forces 19:11–21 *Arrival of the Conquering King of Kings 19:11–16* *Preparation for the Final Slaughter 19:17–19* *The Enemies' Defeat & Consignment to the Lake of Fire 19:20–21* The Binding of Satan 20:1–3 The Thousand-Year Reign of Christ & the Saints 20:4–6	Satan's Failed Final Rebellion & His Final Judgment 20:7–10 The Great White Throne Judgment 20:11–15	The Sight of the New Heaven & the New Earth 21:1 The Descent of the New Jerusalem 21:2 The Banishment of Sorrow from God's Presence 21:3–4 The Divine Promise of Everlasting Joy for Overcomers & Exclusion for Evildoers 21:5–8

THE FOURTH VISION, 21:9–22:5

CONCLUSION, 22:6–21

CHART 68: Focus on Revelation 21:9–22:21

INTRODUCTION, 1:1–8	BODY OF THE BOOK: FOUR HEAVENLY VISIONS 1:9–22:5						CONCLUSION: JOHN'S INVITATION & CHRIST'S FINAL WORDS 22:6–21			
	THE FIRST VISION, 1:9–3:22	THE SECOND VISION, 4:1–16:21	THE THIRD VISION, 17:1–21:8	THE FOURTH VISION: THE NEW CREATION & THE ETERNAL STATE 21:9–22:5						
				The New Jerusalem: The Eternal Temple 21:9–27		**The New Heaven & the New Earth: Paradise Restored 22:1–5**	**First Round of Christ's Final Words 22:6–9**	**Second Round of Christ's Final Words 22:10–15**	**Third Round of Christ's Final Words 22:16–17**	**Fourth Round of Christ's Final Words 22:18–21**
				Description of the City's Surpassing Beauty 21:9–21 The New Jerusalem Described as Christ's Bride 21:9 The Descent of the New Jerusalem, the Gleaming City with Twelve Gates 21:10–14 The City's Massive Measurements 21:15–17 The Precious Composition of Its Construction 21:18–21	**Description of the City's Consummate Holiness 21:22–27** No Temple Needed in the Temple City 21:22 No Light Needed in the Glorious City of Light 21:23–26 No Uncleanness Permitted in the Perfect Place for the Forgiven 21:27	The River of Life & the Tree of Life 22:1–2 The Elimination of the Curse & the Night 22:3–5	Angelic Validation of the Prophecy 22:6 Christ's Promise of Return & Blessing 22:7 John's Mistaken Adulation of the Angel 22:8–9	Angelic Instruction Not to Seal the Relevant Book 22:10–11 Christ's Promise of Return & Reward 22:12–13 John's Blessing on Those Who Inherit the City 22:14–15	Jesus' Validation of the Book's Message to the Churches 22:16 John's Relay of Invitation from the Spirit & the Bride 22:17	John's Warning Not to Alter the Prophecy 22:18–19 Jesus' Testimony of the Book & His Promise to Come Soon 22:20a John's Prayer for Jesus' Soon Coming 22:20b John's Closing Prayer of Grace 22:21

Charts 69–72 pertain to matters of New Testament chronology and canonical arrangement, and a key Old Testament text to which NT writers very often allude or quote at length.

Chart 69 displays the traditional arrangement of NT writings used for most of the last millennium. The arrangement came to be ordered by genre, authorship, and word count. The word count of Greek words in Paul's letters shows how they were arranged almost entirely according to length, not their order of composition.

Chart 70 lists out the order in which NT books may have been written. The early dating attributed to Matthew reflects a somewhat traditional understanding of the authorship and occasions behind the Synoptic Gospels. The chart also sets forth the likely location of each book's author and recipients, and a brief statement about circumstances pertaining to its purpose or setting.

Chart 71 details a chronology of Paul's life and service, showing how his inscripturated writings fit into the second half of his Christian life. The dates of the crucifixion and the Jerusalem Council are debated and must be correlated with details in the gospels, Acts and Paul's epistles to establish a coherent chronology. This chart sets the crucifixion date around AD 30 and the Jerusalem Council in AD 49.

Chart 72 sets forth the purpose and structure of Isaiah 52:13–53:12. This messianic oracle, one of Isaiah's so-called "Servant Songs," is of tremendous importance to NT writers. The NT alludes to or quotes this passage more often than any other extended portion in the OT (though the most referenced OT verse is Psalm 110:1). NT writers consistently see its direct fulfilment in Jesus Christ. In the chart I have inserted my own translation or explanation of a few phrases to clarify the meaning of this complex and profoundly important poem.

CHART 69
The Traditional Arrangement of New Testament Books

©2016 M. Scott Bashoor

The books of the New Testament are arranged based upon their genres, the authors' identity or prominence, the length of the materials, the recipients, and, on rare occasion, the chronological order of their writing. The current order of the books follows the majority tradition of the past millennium, but it is not original or inspired.

HISTORICAL BOOKS		EPISTLES BY APOSTLES AND ASSOCIATED PROPHETS								
THE LIFE OF JESUS	THE EARLY CHURCH	EPISTLES BY PAUL				EPISTLES BY OTHER WRITERS				
		Letters to Churches		Letters to Leaders		Disputed Author		Regional Encyclicals & Local Letters		Prophetic Encyclical
		Letter's Recipient	*Word Count*	Letter's Recipient	*Word Count*	Letter's Recipient	*Word Count*	Letter's Author	*Word Count*	
Matthew 18,363 words to Jews		**Romans**	*7,114*	**1 Timothy**	*1,591*	**Hebrews**	*4,956*	*First Non-Apostolic Epistle*		**Revelation** 9,856 words
Mark 11,312 words to Gentiles		**1 Corinthians**	*6,841*	**2 Timothy**	*1,239*					
Luke 19,495 words to a Gentile	**Acts** 18,470 words to a Gentile	**2 Corinthians**	*4,488*	**Titus**	*659*			**James**	*1,746*	
		Galatians	*2,233*					*Peter's Letters*	*2,779*	
John 15,671 words to Jews		*Prison Epistles*		**Philemon**	*335*			**1 Peter**	*1,680*	
		Ephesians	*2,423*					**2 Peter**	*1,099*	
		Philippians	*1,631*					*John's Letters*	*2,603*	
		Colossians	*1,581*					**1 John**	*2,140*	
		1 Thessalonians	*1,482*					**2 John**	*245*	
		2 Thessalonians	*823*					**3 John**	*218*	
								Last Non-Apostolic Epistle		
								Jude	*458*	

Greek word count based on the *Novum Testamentum Graeca*, NA[28] revised ©2012 Accordance Bible Software.

Chart 70 Chronological Order of New Testament Books

Book	Date	Origination	Recipients	Circumstances
James	c. 40–45	Palestine	Jewish Christians	Readers are dispersed in Palestine & Syria under duress
Galatians	49	Corinth	Gentile churches in Galatia	Judaizers have made incursions; the Jerusalem Council follows
Matthew	c. 50	Syria	Syrian Jews/Jewish Christians	Written to assure Hellenistic Jews of Jesus' Kingship
1 Thess.	51	Corinth	Gentile Christians in Thessalonica	Paul explains his absence and corrects false notions about the end times
2 Thess.	51	Corinth	Gentile Christians in Thessalonica	Paul learns months later his first letter was only partially heeded
1 Cor.	55	Ephesus	Mostly Gentile Christians in Corinth	After several years away from Corinth, Paul learns of major problems
2 Cor.	55	Philippi	Mostly Gentile Christians in Corinth	Paul prepares to visit again, sending this letter to prepare the way
Romans	56	Corinth	Gentile & Jewish Christians in Rome	Paul instructs the church on unity in the gospel & prepares for a visit
Luke	c. 60–61	Caesarea?	An Influential Gentile named Theophilus	Explains how Jesus' life & sacrifice were God's plan for mankind
Ephesians	61	Rome	Gentile churches around Ephesus	Paul instructs Gentiles on their calling into the church & to holiness
Colossians	61	Rome	The Gentile church of Colossae	Paul instructs Gentiles on their holy calling into union with Christ
Philemon	61	Rome	A Christian slave owner in Colossae	Paul returns an escaped slave & urges him to be accepted as a brother
Philippians	62	Rome	Gentile Church in Philippi	Paul thanks them for their generosity & encourages stronger unity
Acts	63	Rome	Influential Gentile named Theophilus	Luke shows how Paul's Gentile ministry continued that of Peter & Jesus
Mark	c. 64–68	Rome	Gentile Romans	Reflects the preaching & teaching of Peter, under whom Mark served
1 Peter	c. 64–65	Rome	Gentile churches of Anatolia	Encourages believers facing growing pressure & hostility
1 Timothy	65	Macedonia	Timothy at Ephesus	Timothy is endorsed to reform the church in Paul's stead
Titus	65	On the move	Titus on Crete	Paul endorses Titus to continue forming the new churches on the isle
2 Timothy	c. 67–68	Rome	Timothy at Ephesus	Paul advises Timothy about ministry priorities & calls for his help
Hebrews	c. 67–69	Unknown	Hebrews Christians in Rome	Urges Christian faith/faithfulness apart from the legal safety of Judaism
2 Peter	c. 68–69	Rome	Gentile churches of Anatolia	Warns of a coming surge of false teaching
Jude	c. 69	Unknown	Anatolia?	Strengthens churches amid the surge of false teaching
John	c. 80–90	Ephesus	Jews in the Dispersion	Fills in details of Jesus life not listed by the other gospels
1, 2, 3 John	c. 90–95	Ephesus	Churches in Asia Minor	Churches are reeling after an exodus led by false teachers
Revelation	c. 94–96	Isle of Patmos	7 Churches of Asia Minor	Challenges 7 churches about their present state & things to come

CHART 71 Select Timeline of Paul's Life and Letters

Year	**c. 5 BC–AD 6**	**AD 22–AD ??**	**c. AD 32**	**c. AD 33–34**	**c. AD 34**	**c. AD 35–37**	**AD 37**	**AD 37–46**	**AD 46**	**AD 46–47**
Events	Born in Tarsus	Studies Under Gamaliel	Assists in Stephen's Martyrdom	Converted on road to Damascus	Begins Preaching in Damascus	Discipled by Jesus in Arabia	Introduced to Jerusalem Church	Ministers in Tarsus for Ten Years	Ministers in Antioch One Year	First Mission-ary Journey
Notes & Refs.	Acts 9:11	Acts 22:3	Acts 7:54–8:3 *Assumes* c. *AD 30 as Crucifixion date*	Acts 9:1–19; Gal 1:15–17	Acts 9:23–25; 2 Cor 11:32–33	Gal 1:11–12, 16–17	Acts 9:26; Gal 1:18	Acts 9:30; 11:25	Acts 11:25	Acts 13–14

Year	**AD 49**	**AD 49–51**	**AD 52–57**	**AD 57–59**	**AD 60**	**AD 60–63**	**c. AD 63**	**c. AD 65**	**c. AD 66**	**c. AD 67–68**
Events	The Jerusalem Council	Second Mission-ary Journey	Third Mission-ary Journey	Arrested in Jerusalem; Impri-soned in Caesarea	To Rome for Imperial Trial	First Roman Imprison-ment & Imperial Trials	Wins Case & Released	Ministers around the Aegean	Arrested Again in Troas?	Second Roman Imprison-ment, Imperials Trials & Martyrdom
Epistles Written	Galatians	1 Thess. AD 51 2 Thess. AD 51	1 Cor. AD 55 2 Cor. AD 55 Romans AD 56			Ephesians AD 61 Colossians AD 61 Philemon AD 61 Philippians AD 62		1 Timothy Titus		2 Timothy
Notes & Refs.	Acts 15:1–21 Gal 2:1–10 *Before the Jerusalem Council*	Acts 15:40–18:22 *Acts 16:6	Acts 18:23–21:26	Acts 21:27–26:32	Acts 27:1–28:14	Acts 28:30–31	Phil 1:25 Phlm 22	1 Tim 1:3	2 Tim 4:13–20	2 Tim 4:6

CHART 72 The Gospel According to Isaiah 52:13–53:12

Proposition: Isaiah 52:13–53:12 reveals with great surprise God's prophetic plan to bring ultimate salvation to His people through the punishing death and victory of His Servant.

Author: Isaiah ben Amoz, prophet in Jerusalem
Date: Perhaps after the Assyrian siege of 702 BC
Context: Isaiah 40–66 mostly contains prophecies of hope for Jews in the later Babylonian captivity. This oracle is placed in this middle of that collection.

THE UNLIKELY EXALTATION OF THE SERVANT 52:13–15

He will have Most Honorable Status
52:13

The Wisest Leader "Watch, My Servant will act wisely."
(translation by MSB)

The Highest Glory

He had a Most Horrible Appearance
52:14

His Sufferings as Shocking as were the Nation's "you" = "My people"

His Sufferings Disfiguring as if Not a Man

He Made a Most Amazing Accomplishment
52:15

World-wide Redemption Accomplished

World-wide Renown Achieved

THE UNBELIEVABLE SUFFERING OF THE SERVANT 53:1–9

His Sufferings were Misunderstood 53:1–3

His Endorsement was Disbelieved
53:1

An Unbelievable Message

An Inconceivable Deliverance

His Credentials were Dismissed
53:2

His Improbable Beginning

An Implied Image of Royalty

An Amplified Image of Vulnerability

His Unpromising Development

His Sufferings were Misinterpreted
53:3

His Sufferings were Misinterpreted as Defeat

His Sufferings were Misinterpreted Due to Disgrace

His Sufferings were Undeserved 53:4–6

He Carried Away the Weight of Our Sins
53:4

The Reality of His Work

The Rejection of His Work

He Was Crushed by the Weight of Our Sins
53:5

His Sufferings were Designed to Take Away Our Punishment

His Sufferings Were Designed to Bring About Our Peace

He Was Convicted for Our Waywardness
53:6

The Human Root of His Sufferings: Our Sin

The Divine Reason for His Sufferings: God's Wrath

His Sufferings Were Deliberate 53:7–9

He Suffered as a Willing Victim
53:7

Demonstrated by His Refusal to Complain

Illustrated by the Obedience of Sheep

He Suffered under Extreme Justice
53:8

The Verdicts of Men were Extremely Unjust

The Court of Law was a Travesty of Injustice

The Court of Opinion was a Tragedy of Indifference

The Judgment of God was Extremely Unique

He Suffered according to Divine Design
53:9

His Burial Suggests He was Worthy of Honor

His Conduct Reveals He was Flawless in Character

THE UNEXPECTED EXPLANATION FOR THE SERVANT 53:10–12

The Sufferings of His Soul were According to God's Pleasure
53:10

God Pleased to Accept the Servant as an Offering for Sin

"Though the Lord was pleased *to* afflict him by crushing him, once his soul presents *itself as* a guilt offering, …"
(translation by MSB)

God Pleased to Reward the Servant with the Blessings of Life

The Sufferings of His Soul Brought about Our Salvation
53:11

His Work Finished & Fully Satisfying

His Work Perfect & Fully Justifying

The Sufferings of His Soul Earned His Reward
53:12

The Substance of His Reward: The Mass of People He Redeemed

"Therefore, I will divvy up for Him the many as *His* portion, and He will divvy up the masses as *His* plunder."
(translation by MSB)

The Reason for His Reward: The Depth of the Sacrifice He Made

Translation by M. Scott Bashoor (MSB).

BIBLIOGRAPHY

Akin, Daniel L. *1, 2, 3 John.* New American Commentary 38. Nashville: B&H, 2001.

Allen, David L. *Hebrews.* New American Commentary 35. Nashville: B&H, 2010.

Bateman, Herbert W., IV. *Charts on the Book of Hebrews.* Kregel Charts of the Bible. Grand Rapids: Kregel Academic, 2012.

Barker, Kenneth L., ed. *The NIV Study Bible.* Grand Rapids: Zondervan, 2011.

Beale, G. K. *The Book of Revelation: A Commentary on the Greek Text.* New International Greek Testament Commentary. Grand Rapids: Eerdmans, 1999.

Bock, Darrell L. *Luke: 1:1–9:50.* Baker Exegetical Commentary on the New Testament. Grand Rapids: Baker Academic, 1994.

———. *Luke: 9:51–24:53.* Baker Exegetical Commentary on the New Testament. Grand Rapids: Baker Academic, 1996.

Blomberg, Craig. *Matthew.* New American Commentary 22. Nashville: B&H, 1992.

Borchert, Gerald L. *John 1–11.* New American Commentary 25A. Nashville: B&H, 1996.

———. *John 12–21.* New American Commentary 25B. Nashville: B&H, 2002.

Brooks, James A. *Mark.* New American Commentary 23. Nashville: B&H, 1991.

Bruce, F. F. *The Epistle to the Galatians: A Commentary on the Greek Text.* New International Greek Testament Commentary. Grand Rapids: Eerdmans, 1982.

———. *The Epistle to the Hebrews.* New International Commentary on the New Testament. Grand Rapids: Eerdmans, 1990.

Carson, D. A., ed. *The NIV Zondervan Study Bible.* Grand Rapids: Zondervan, 2015.

Carson, D. A., R. T. France, J. A. Motyer, and G. J. Wenham, eds. *New Bible Commentary: 21st Century Edition.* Downers Grove: Inter-Varsity, 1994.

Cockerill, Gareth Lee. *The Epistle to the Hebrews.* New International Commentary on the New Testament. Grand Rapids: Eerdmans, 2012.

Crossway Bibles. *The ESV Study Bible.* Wheaton: Crossway, 2008.

Davids, Peter H. *The Epistle of James: A Commentary on the Greek Text.* New International Greek Testament Commentary. Grand Rapids: Eerdmans, 1982.

Derickson, Gary W. *First, Second, and Third John.* Evangelical Exegetical Commentary. Bellingham: Lexham, 2012.

deSilva, David A. *Perseverance in Gratitude: A Socio-Rhetorical Commentary on the Epistle "To the Hebrews."* Grand Rapids: Eerdmans, 2000.

Dunn, James D. G. *The Epistles to the Colossians and to Philemon: A Commentary on the Greek Text.* New International Greek Testament Commentary. Grand Rapids: Eerdmans, 1996.

Ellingworth, Paul. *The Epistle to the Hebrews: A Commentary on the Greek Text.* New International Greek Testament Commentary. Grand Rapids: Eerdmans, 1993.

Essex. Keith H. "BI 601. New Testament Studies: Course Notes." Unpublished course materials. The Master's Seminary. Los Angeles, 2015.

Fanning, Buist M., III. *Revelation.* Zondervan Exegetical Commentary on the New Testament. Edited by Clinton E. Arnold. Grand Rapids: Zondervan, 2020.

France, R. T. *The Gospel of Mark: A Commentary on the Greek Text.* New International Greek Testament Commentary. Grand Rapids: Eerdmans, 2002.

Garland, David E. *1 Corinthians.* Baker Exegetical Commentary on the New Testament. Grand Rapids: Baker Academic, 2003.

Garland, David E. *2 Corinthians.* New American Commentary 29. Nashville: B&H, 1999.

Gaebelein, Frank E., ed. *The Expositor's Bible Commentary.* 12 vols. Grand Rapids: Zondervan, 1984.

George, Timothy. *Galatians.* New American Commentary 30. Nashville: B&H, 1994.

Harris, Murray J. *The Second Epistle to the Corinthians: A Commentary on the Greek Text.* New International Greek Testament Commentary. Grand Rapids: Eerdmans, 2005.

Hindson, Edward E., ed. *King James Version Study Bible.* Nashville: Thomas Nelson, 1997.

Holman Bible Editorial Staff. *HCSB Study Bible: God's Word for Life.* Nashville: Holman Bible, 2010.

House, H. Wayne. *Chronological and Background Charts of the New Testamen*t. 2nd ed. Grand Rapids: Zondervan, 2009.

Hughes, Philip Edgcumbe. *A Commentary on the Epistle to the Hebrews.* New International Commentary on the New Testament. Grand Rapids: Eerdmans, 1977.

Jobes, Karen H. *1 Peter.* Baker Exegetical Commentary on the New Testament. Grand Rapids: Baker Academic, 2005.

Kierspel, Lars. *Charts on the Life, Letters, and Theology of Paul.* Kregel Charts of the Bible. Grand Rapids: Kregel Academic, 2012.

Knight, George W. *The Pastoral Epistles: A Commentary on the Greek Text.* New International Greek Testament Commentary. Grand Rapids: Eerdmans, 1992.

Köstenberger, Andreas J. *John.* Baker Exegetical Commentary on the New Testament. Grand Rapids: Baker Academic, 2004.

Lane, William L. *Hebrews 1–8.* Word Biblical Commentary 47A. Dallas: Word, 1998.

———. *Hebrews 9–13.* Word Biblical Commentary 47B. Dallas: Word, 1998.

Lea, Thomas D., and Hayne P. Griffin. *1, 2 Timothy, Titus.* New American Commentary 34. Nashville: B&H, 1992.

MacArthur, John, Jr., ed. *The MacArthur Study Bible: New King James Version.* Nashville: Word, 1997.

Marshall, I. Howard. *The Gospel of Luke: A Commentary on the Greek Text.* New International Greek Testament Commentary. Grand Rapids: Eerdmans, 1978.

Martin, D. Michael. *1, 2 Thessalonians.* New American Commentary 33. Nashville: B&H, 1995.

Melick, Richard R. *Philippians, Colossians, Philemon.* New American Commentary 32. Nashville: B&H, 1991.

Moo, Douglas J. *The Epistle to the Romans.* New International Commentary on the New Testament. Grand Rapids: Eerdmans, 1996.

———. *The Letter of James.* Pillar New Testament Commentary. Grand Rapids: Eerdmans, 2000.

Mounce, Robert H. *Romans.* New American Commentary 27. Nashville: B&H, 1995.

Motyer, Alec. *The Prophecy of Isaiah: An Introduction & Commentary.* Downers Grove: InterVarsity Press, 1993.

Nolland, John. *The Gospel of Matthew: A Commentary on the Greek Text.* New International Greek Testament Commentary. Grand Rapids: Eerdmans, 2005.

O'Brien, Peter Thomas. *The Epistle to the Philippians: A Commentary on the Greek Text.* New International Greek Testament Commentary. Grand Rapids: Eerdmans, 1991.

Osborne, Grant R. *Revelation.* Baker Exegetical Commentary on the New Testament. Grand Rapids: Baker Academic, 2002.

Oswalt, John N. *The Book of Isaiah: Chapters 40-66.* The New International Commentary on the Old Testament. Grand Rapids: Eerdmans, 1998.

Patterson, Paige. *Revelation.* New American Commentary 39. Nashville: B&H, 2012.

Polhill, John B. *Acts.* New American Commentary 26. Nashville: B&H, 1992.

Richardson, Kurt A. *James.* New American Commentary 36. Nashville: B&H, 1997.

Schreiner, Thomas R. *1, 2 Peter, Jude.* New American Commentary 37. Nashville: B&H, 2003.

Schreiner, Thomas R. *Romans.* Baker Exegetical Commentary on the New Testament. Grand Rapids: Baker Academic, 1998.

Silva, Moisés. *Philippians.* 2nd ed. Baker Exegetical Commentary on the New Testament. Grand Rapids: Baker Academic, 2005.

Sproul, R. C., ed. *The Reformation Study Bible.* Orlando: Reformation Trust, 2015.

Stein, Robert H. *Luke.* New American Commentary 24. Nashville: B&H, 1992.

Sweeney, Marvin A. *Isaiah 40–66.* Forms of the Old Testament Literature 19. Grand Rapids: Eerdmans, 2016.

Thiselton, Anthony C. *The First Epistle to the Corinthians: A Commentary on the Greek Text.* New International Greek Testament Commentary. Grand Rapids: Eerdmans, 2000.

Thomas, Robert L. *Revelation 1–7: An Exegetical Commentary.* Chicago: Moody, 1992.

———. *Revelation 8–22: An Exegetical Commentary.* Chicago: Moody, 1995.

Towner, Philip H. *The Letters to Timothy and Titus.* New International Commentary of the New Testament. Grand Rapids: Eerdmans, 2006.

Varner, William. *James: A Commentary on the Greek Text.* Dallas: Fontes, 2017.

Walvoord, John F., and Roy B. Zuck, eds. *The Bible Knowledge Commentary: An Exposition of the Scriptures by Dallas Seminary Faculty: New Testament.* Wheaton: Victor Books, 1985.

Wanamaker, Charles A. *The Epistles to the Thessalonians: A Commentary on the Greek Text.* New International Greek Testament Commentary. Grand Rapids: Eerdmans, 1990.

Whitlock, Luder G., R. C. Sproul, Bruce K. Waltke, and Moisés Silva, eds. *The Reformation Study Bible: New King James Version.* Nashville: Thomas Nelson, 1995.

Wilson, Mark. *Charts on the Book of Revelation: Literary, Historical, and Theological Perspectives.* Kregel Charts of the Bible and Theology. Grand Rapids: Kregel Academic, 2007.

Young, Edward. *The Book of Isaiah.* Grand Rapids: Eerdmans, 1972.

ABOUT THE AUTHOR

M. Scott Bashoor is a Faculty Associate in the Old Testament and Bible divisions at The Master's University and Seminary (Los Angeles). He has also pastored in Orange County for over 20 years and is currently co-pastor of Community Bible Church (Anaheim). In addition to VOCNT, his publications include articles and essays on Bible interpretation, pastoral ministry, and preaching. Scott earned a B.A. from Bob Jones University and an M.Div. and Th.M. from The Master's Seminary where he is currently pursuing a Ph.D. He is a member of the Evangelical Theological Society.

www.ingramcontent.com/pod-product-compliance
Lightning Source LLC
Chambersburg PA
CBHW041959150426
43194CB00002B/64

* 9 7 8 0 9 8 6 4 4 4 2 5 8 *